the Multiples manual

Preparing and Caring for TWINS or TRIPLETS

1,002 Tips for Expectant Mothers

Lynn Lorenz

THE MULTIPLES MANUAL

Preparing and Caring for Twins or Triplets
1,002 Tips for Expectant Mothers

~2nd Edition~

By Lynn Lorenz

Copyright ©2007 by JustMultiples.com, LLC
www.justmultiples.com

ISBN#: 0-9724676-3-7

Illustrations by Shelley Dieterichs

My mother at a county fair representing
the Raritan Bay Mothers of Multiples Club, 1970.

DEDICATION

....

This manual is dedicated to my mother. She is a mother of multiples who did her best without sonograms, nutrition information, a minivan, car seats, disposable diapers, baby swings, bouncy seats, and books full of tips to help her prepare for twins or triplets! In fact, my mother had no idea she was having twins until an x-ray was taken two weeks before her due date. Can you imagine her surprise?

"Uh...you know that weight gain I've been concerned about? Well... it's another fetus, not water retention, as I have been suggesting for the past few months. You might want to stop and pick up a few more baby products on your way home...oh, and by the way, congratulations!"

As you read this manual, envision my mother and what her challenges must have been with twins in 1965, and be thankful for the modern conveniences we now enjoy.

ACKNOWLEDGEMENTS

The following are those I would like to thank for their encouragement, suggestions and support:

- My husband, Fred
- My triplets, Jeffrey, Drew and Karlie
- My singleton, Brooke
- My twin sister, Lisa
- My sister, Kris
- My mother, Jill, and father, Richard
- My aunt, "Tante" Bea
- My friend and fellow mother of multiples, Cathy
- My J&J co-workers, Arlene, Jeff, Karen, Liz and Terri
- My Just Multiples co-workers, Anette and Karen
- My friend, Sandy, owner of Double Blessings
- The Greater Montgomery Mothers of Multiples
- Central Jersey Triplets and More
- Raritan Valley Mothers of Multiples
- Mothers of multiples friends in addition to the clubs I have mentioned
- Hubie, for her creative ability and friendship
- Taster's Choice instant coffee

CONTENTS

ABOUT THE AUTHOR

Lynn Lorenz (top) is an identical twin, mother of triplets (two boys, one girl) and a singleton girl. She has been actively involved with various Mothers of Multiples organizations and has held officer positions with Central Jersey Triplets and More and the Greater Montgomery Mothers of Multiples. She has been a member of the National Organization of Twins Mothers Clubs, Triplet Connection and Mothers of Supertwins (MOST). Lynn is also the creator and owner of Just Multiples *(www.justmultiples.com)*, a website offering a variety of products for twins, triplets and their families.

Lynn lives in Pennington, New Jersey with her four children and husband Fred, a financial advisor and contributor to *The Multiples Manual.* Her twin sister, Lisa, lives about an hour away (close, yet far enough away so that they no longer share the same shadow, or steal each others' clothing).

DEAR EXPECTANT MOMS,

As you read *The Multiples Manual,* keep in mind that I am a person who has "been there, done that," but I am not a medical professional. Please consult your health-care provider if you have questions regarding anyone's health or safety.

Please also note that the contents in this book are intended to provide helpful tips for expectant mothers of twins or triplets. Although there are products, companies and websites mentioned in this manual, not one of them is a paid advertisement.

If you have any feedback on *The Multiples Manual,* I would like to hear from you. Your input will help to improve future editions of this book. Please send an e-mail to *justmultiples@yahoo.com* with your comments.

Best Wishes,

Lynn Lorenz
justmultiples@yahoo.com
www.justmultiples.com

FORWARD (THINKING?)

"I'm *WHAT*?"

"You're pregnant."

"You're kidding, right?"

"I'm not kidding. We need to schedule a sonogram to confirm how many sacs there are. Your HCG levels suggest there may be more than one."

"*More* than one?

"I can't possibly be pregnant with more than one baby! This doctor must have mistaken me for someone else," I thought. "How can I go from 'no such luck' for so long, to *multiples*? The only luck I ever had was back in the 80s when I won a frozen Butterball turkey at a high school football game! I also won a few dollars in Atlantic City once or twice, but this is different. If it's true, this luck will change my life forever!"

And it did. After months of gloating and shopping, the "big day" finally arrived. I had a caesarean section delivery, and within one minute, three beautiful babies were born. By the next minute, I stared like a deer in the headlights as a team of highly trained doctors and nurses raced around the operating room attending to each baby's every need. By the third minute I wondered, "How on earth will I be able care for these babies without a staff of professionals to help me? This looks like more work than I anticipated, not to mention, it's been at least 15 years since I babysat or changed a diaper!"

After "winging it" for the first year or so (without the highly trained hospital staff), I finally figured out what I was doing and came to this conclusion: I should have spent more of my "gestation" time learning about how to prepare and care for multiples, and less time agonizing over what color to paint the nursery! Yes indeed, hindsight was 20/20.

Since those delirious days, I have spent much of my time writing *The Multiples Manual* to help lucky women like you prepare for the fun, excitement and challenges that lie ahead. There is one thing to keep in mind when reading *The Multiples Manual* — this book is full of suggestions, not rules to live by. Always remember that what works best is what works for you and your family. There is no "wrong" way of doing something unless advised against by a medical professional. There can also be a hundred "right" ways of doing something!

I have formatted this book to follow a general timeline. Although this book covers topics including childproofing and preschool, these contain information which should be understood *before or shortly after you give birth*, to prepare you in advance of reaching a particular milestone. There are some chapters that you might want to skim over initially, and go back to and read in more detail when the timing is more appropriate. For example, you won't want to read everything there is to know about strollers until you are ready to shop for one (otherwise the chapter may bore you to tears), and you might want to skip over the breastfeeding chapter if you already bought, sterilized and color coded hundreds of bottles!

As you read through this manual, grab a pen or highlighter and mark the tips you might find useful. This will make them easier to refer back to as you need them.

Since we have 1,002 tips to discuss, let's get started. I know your free time is limited!

ME AND MY SHADOW(S)

People often ask me, "What is the best part about being a twin?" My response has always been, "I could write a book!" For as long as I can remember, just about every fond memory I have has a vivid picture of my identical twin sister, Lisa, sharing the moment with me. I can't imagine what my life would be like without my sidekick. In an effort to answer this question without writing a novel about it, I will simply say this: The best part about *being* a twin is…*having* a twin! Realize that not only is your multiple pregnancy extraordinary, so too is the special bond of friendship your multiples will likely share.

• • •

Growing up, my best friend was, and still is, my twin sister. We had the same friends, same teachers, same grades, same bedroom, wore matching clothing, you name it, it matched. Today we continue to share. We jointly own a twin-engine boat that we named the "Twin Thing" (silly,

I know, but we couldn't resist)! Although we have the same mannerisms, and are spitting images of one another, we never shared a secret language, or had a sense of what the other was doing, thinking, or feeling. As I write this, I have no idea whether Lisa is happy or sad, nor do I know what she might be doing. There are numerous theories on this subject known as "cryptophasia," and many parents of multiples are intrigued by it. My theory is that secret languages do not exist. Expect your multiples to babble with each other while they are babies, and to share a special bond, but don't be disappointed if they're not telepathic! *NOTE: To read more about "telepathic" twins, visit* www.twinconnections.com.

• • •

Parents are often concerned about their children's individuality because people often refer to them as the "twins" or "triplets" and not by name. What parents sometimes don't realize are two things: 1) It may be difficult for people to know, or remember "who is who" unless they tattoo names on their foreheads (you may find this to be the case with identical and fraternal multiples, especially while they are young); and 2) Multiples often enjoy being referred to as "twins" or "triplets" because it gives them a sense of notoriety. Since there won't be much you can do about what others call your children, don't let this bother you. If it does, ask family members to call them by name (assuming they can tell them apart). If you give this a bit more thought, is it all that different from parents referring to their singletons as the "kids"? For whatever it's worth, I consider myself to be very independent, and I was rarely "Lynn" but "twin."

• • •

Don't expect that most people will be able to tell your multiples apart, even when you venture out with a girl and boy dressed in pink and blue! You will be amazed at how "gender-neutral" some people can be. Whenever I dressed my triplets in pink and blue, people continued to ask, "Are they boys or girls?" "The two dressed in blue with the fire trucks on their shirts are boys, and the one in pink with the bow in her hair is a girl." G-e-e-z-e! Well, I guess I shouldn't complain. My own grandfather could never tell me apart from my sister, even after his cataract surgery! I guess we didn't see him often enough for him to figure out who was who. Also, I can't tell you how many times my brother-in-law briefly mistakes me for my sister. Luckily, he has yet to plant a big wet kiss on me, but I am armed and ready when the day comes!

• • •

You may also be totally impressed by the insightful ability of others. I have a blind-from-birth cousin who amazes me. After months of not seeing her, I can walk into a room without speaking a word, and she always says, "Hi Lynn!" with the utmost of confidence. Somehow she uses her other senses to tell me apart from my sister. To this day I can't figure out how she does it. Do I drag my feet when I walk? Do I have bad breath, or a certain body odor? I don't know (perhaps my sister does). Nevertheless, my cousin has such fun telling us apart without sharing her secret.

• • •

When my triplets were babies, they were known as the "triplets" for obvious reasons. They all sat, similar in size, in a triple stroller whenever we ventured out. Unless someone saw them everyday, it would have been difficult for anyone to determine who was who especially since they all looked like Winston Churchill. Don't all babies look like that man? Now that my children are older, this is no longer the case. Today, someone might notice that we are with a group of kids that are about the same age, but rarely does anyone comment on the fact that we have triplets (although someone once asked if I ran a daycare center). So, the good news is parents of fraternal multiples have little to worry about on the subject of individuality, particularly as their children grow and develop as individuals.

• • •

If you are concerned about your multiples maintaining their own iden- tity, whether you dress them alike or not is probably not going to matter. I have met scores of women who wonder if they are "doing the right thing" when dressing their children. I have two suggestions for you: 1) Do whatever you think is right, not what everyone else thinks; and 2) Don't become a "matching maniac" like a woman I know from my multiples club (I hope she doesn't read this!). This mother has triplet girls and insists on matching her daughters every day, all day. I am talking 24 hours a day, 7 days a week, 365 days a year. Each girl's outfit *always* looks just like the next, and the comical part is when one girl soils her clothing, *all* of them get changed! Don't get me wrong, I think matching is cute and can be fun, but don't feel the need to clone your clan every minute of the day. If you do, you are creating work for yourself, and others are bound to make fun of you!

• • •

My twin and I were dressed alike most of the time, and I didn't mind the matching outfits. In fact, I can't recall having any opinion at all about whether I liked the "twin thing" or not. What I did mind was the hair-sprayed bun and baloney curls my mother would create on top of our heads. The hair was pulled so tight, but the worst part was that I could look at my sister and see how ridiculous I looked! Another suggestion: If you are going to match your multiples, do so with some fashion sense! Other than that, don't think twice about it.

• • •

Just pray that your multiples don't someday turn into the Dunkleberger twins! Esther and Alfreda Dunkleberger were not just any old identical twins (God rest their similar souls). They were my grandmother's flaky friends who could always be found sitting side-by-side on her couch sharing tea and vanilla cookies whenever I came for a visit. Everything about them was identical — their looks, clothing, wrinkled stockings, shoes, purses, matching earrings, necklaces, rings, nail polish, lipstick color, and even dress pins were strategically placed! Of course, their hair was the same style and hue of gray-blue, right down to the location of the bobby pins that held their hair in place. Esther and Alfreda lived together, and when Esther finally got married, Alfreda moved in with her sister and new hubby. At first I found this strange, but the more I thought about it, their living arrangement actually made sense: How else would they coordinate clothing and accessories?

• • •

Keep them together, or apart, it doesn't matter (unless you're a Dunkle-berger!). The separation issue is another subject that some parents worry about, but shouldn't. A child is not going to grow up with a nervous twitch because he didn't sleep in the same room with his twin when he was two, although some parents might develop one if they think too much about it! My twin and I had so much "togetherness" when we were young that at one point I began to believe my shadow really had four legs and two heads. It was nice to get a "breather" from her every now and then. Here's my best analogy of how I often felt: Have you ever spent so much time with your husband that you thought it might be nice if he took a little trip somewhere, if only for a weekend? A couple days "apart" would enable you to have stress-free potato chip dinners, and some extra time to thumb though your piles of *People* magazines without guilt or interruption. The fact is we all need a little break every now and then. This includes spouses…and twins!

. . .

If your multiples are identical, they will always be identical, no matter what you do. My sister and I have never truly had our own identity. I will never forget the day I sat in a pizzeria for one of the first times without my sister. I was in college and noticed a table of boys who kept staring at me. I was flattered until one of them approached me and asked, "Are you Lisa?" When I told him I was "Lynn, not Lisa," he must have thought he had discovered a set of twins who had been separated at birth, considering I was more than 400 miles from my sister! As it turned out, the boys went to the same college as my sister and had been visiting my school for a football game. Today, my sister lives about an hour from me, and I am amazed at the number of people I have never met who approach me with a kiss. On the other hand, I often hear my own friends tell me, "Boy, were you rude yesterday. I saw you at the mall, and you didn't even say hello!"

. . .

A tip for the future: If you have identical twins or triplets, think twice before encouraging them to work together. In high school, my twin and I both worked in an ice cream parlor and before long we were known as the "double dips" to most customers. We also worked as cashiers at Burger King for a while. Since we had to wear matching polyester out-fits, customers got confused and yelled at us all the time. "Hey! Where's my burger? Why are you helping *that* customer and not *me*?" I always enjoyed telling them, "Because you're not my customer!" as I went about my business. I must admit, doing this made my minimum-wage job very rewarding.

. . .

In my opinion, the most significant issue with parenting multiples is how to manage the "attention factor." I can't recall any concerns about my own individuality, but remember my younger sister crying herself to sleep many nights because she was not a "twin." Getting lots of attention as a twin or triplet is one thing, but feeling as though you don't get enough attention is another. Your multiples, just by nature of the fact that they are multiples, will get most of the attention. You will probably find that more often than not, people will approach you and ask, "How are the twins (triplets)?", failing to ask about your other children. Be aware of the hurt feelings this can cause. If you have other children in your family, make an effort to introduce them first whenever you encounter someone, and try to schedule one-on-one time with them whenever possible. When you venture out, ask your other child(ren) to push the stroller so that he/she feels like a "big" brother or sister. Most young children feel good about themselves when they are pleasing their parents, or can do something their siblings can't!

• • •

Speaking of other siblings, don't be so quick to get rid of your children's toys and clothing once they outgrow them. I know many women, myself included, who thought their family was complete with a multiple birth and later decided they would like to have more children. Although this is probably the *last* thing on your mind right now, it is a thought to keep in the archives!

"After having your multiples, be careful if you decide you would like to try again to 'see what's it's like to have one baby.' You might get more than you bargained for!"
— Kathy R. (Mother of two sets of twins and a singleton)

NOTE: *If you have fraternal twins, your chance of having another set quadruples! Most women who conceive fraternal twins (without the help of fertility treatments) show a pattern of releasing more than one egg per cycle, although this is not the case with identical twins.*

IMPERFECT STRANGERS

Expectant mothers are magnets for advice givers. The fact is, when your stomach grows to two or three times the size a typical expectant belly does, your magnetic force seems to be two to three times as great. Everyone will have comments, stories, tips, warnings, words of wisdom, and even well wishes for you. Advice givers come in all shapes and sizes, and they usually offer their two cents (sometimes it's worth three cents) when you least expect it. Some won't always have the time to stop and chat, but they will always feel compelled to say something. I will never forget the day I was walking around town when a jogger (who was a fraction of my size), yelled "Any day now!" as he raced by. When I replied with "Only four more months!," I had to laugh when I saw the confused, sweaty look on his face. Prepare to be the center of attention, and try to have some fun with it.

• • •

Amuse yourself with those who "sense" you are having a girl because you're "wide in the bottom" or a boy, because you're "all stomach." Although there is a chance you will end up wide in the bottom *and* big in the stomach, no one ever "senses" multiples! Lucky for me, I was big and wide everywhere. This included my stomach, butt, neck, hands, shoulders, boobs, and even my ankles. I had "litter" written all over me, but no one ever sensed "two boys and a girl."

• • •

With multiples, giving birth will not put an end to advice giving and comments and in fact, it may make it worse. I will never forget two of my most memorable comments from complete strangers: While my family sat having lunch in a Friendly's restaurant, a man walked in with his wife, pointed at my triplets and shouted, "Modern medicine!" Another zinger was from a woman on a checkout line at Babies "R" Us: "Oh, now I know why you have dark circles under your eyes…you have *triplets!*" In cases like these, you will need a witty comeback line. It is never too early to start thinking of some good ones!

• • •

There are many more good-hearted strangers than there are ignorant ones. You will find their comments to be genuine and kind. These are the people you may end up having brief conversations with. Take these compliments to heart, because they can be very uplifting.

"When I took my triplets to the circus, I got the best comment ever! There was a group of women behind us, and one lady asked if my triplets were 'nocturnal.' I didn't want to embarrass her, but her friend caught on and mocked the heck out of her. She obviously meant to say 'fraternal.' Sometimes you can get a good laugh out of the comments people make."
— Tracey T. (Mother of BBG triplets)

"I was in the cafeteria at work one day waiting to order my lunch. While standing on line, a man from another department turned to me and said, 'I heard you had twins. Were they natural, or did you do fraternity drugs?' If I hadn't been at work, I would have told him, 'Yes, but I didn't inhale,' but instead I asked, 'Did you mean fertility drugs?'"
— Sandra H. (Mother of BB twins)

ExPECTATIONS AND PREPARATION

C harles Dickens, who authored *A Tale of Two Cities,* opens the novel with the line, "It was the best of times, it was the worst of times, it was the age of wisdom, it was the age of foolishness…" Based on his opening, I've often wondered if he were the father of multiples because he perfectly summarized the first year of caring for them! Expect the first 12 months of parenting to be just as Dickens described. When the first year is over, you will realize the best of times far outweighed the worst; you made lots of foolish mistakes along the way, and gained great wisdom from the experience!

• • •

Don't think that because you already have a child, were an expert babysitter, worked your tail off in a daycare center, or have multiple nieces and nephews that you will be able to care for your twins or triplets with few challenges. Having your own children and more than one the same age is an entirely different ballgame. Mothers of multiples are in a league of their own. Only a mother of multiples can feed a hungry baby with her feet, pour formula into a bottle using her teeth, change a diaper using her elbows, and manage to fold laundry at the same time. This is true! Ask anyone else to do it, and they will tell you they can't!

• • •

I created the following chart to summarize the degree of difficulty ("challenges") I faced in the first five years of parenting multiples. I found the challenges to be most difficult in the early months, and parenting to become much easier as the months/years passed (with the exception of the "terrible twos"). This chart offers a general idea of what to expect (but remember that everyone's experience will be somewhat different). *NOTE: The timeframe and degree of difficulty may be quite different for parents who have very premature infants.*

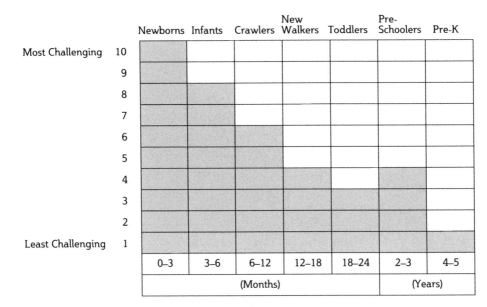

0–3 months: Mom/Dad are inexperienced, exhausted, and may have thoughts of giving their babies up for adoption (just kidding!). Newborns are unpredictable and feeding around the clock. Babies' crying seems constant.

3–6 months: Mom/Dad establish a routine (although their babies haven't) and, for the most part, know what to expect. Infants are sleeping for longer periods at night, but not sleeping through. Crying persists.

6–12 months: Mom/Dad are more confident. Babies are sleeping through the night, but are sometimes wakeful. They are beginning to crawl and are much happier, but they are growing, and carrying them around becomes tiresome.

12–18 months: Babies are interacting/playing with each other and with Mom/Dad. They are just learning to walk and explore their surroundings. Bumps and bruises are frequent.

18–24 months: A relatively simple stage. Toddlers are walking with more confidence and stability and parents no longer have to carry them everywhere.

2–3 years: The "terrible twos (and threes)." Children begin to run in different directions and get into things. They are often difficult to discipline and throw tantrums. Not necessarily a "terrible" stage, but pretty close!

4–5 years: Smooth sailing! Children are much better behaved and are more independent. You might wish you had more children at this stage. *NOTE: Go ahead, have another baby! You're a wonderful mother. Wouldn't it be a blessing to have multiples again?*

"Parenting triplets is a lot of work, but it's so much fun! My children are the loves of my life!" — Kathleen H. (Mother of GBB triplets)

"Keep your sense of humor, no matter how frazzled you become. Now that my twins are older, they enjoy listening to me tell stories of when they were babies. We now laugh hysterically at the many things that used to totally stress me out. In hindsight, just about everything is a crack-up!" — Debbie C. (Mother of 7-year-old BB twins)

YOUR PLURAL PREGNANCY

A woman of childbearing age has a 1 in 90 chance of giving birth to twins (1 in 38 with fertility treatments), and a 1 in 7,000 (1 in 539 with fertility treatments) chance of having triplets. Congratulations on adding by two or three to the world population of 6,525,294,588, and if you live in the United States, even more significantly to its population of 300,000,000! Although there will be challenges ahead, prepare to feel like one of the luckiest people in the world! *NOTE: If you are a mother of fraternal twin girls and conceived without the help of fertility treatments, there is a 12% chance one of your daughters will add to the world population in multiples. This is even higher if you have triplet girls — hold on to those adorable outfits!*

• • •

According to the Centers for Disease Control and Prevention, just about 2.9% of all births in the United States are multiple births — there were 64,335 sets of twins, 2,370 sets of triplets, 117 sets of quadruplets, and 17 sets quintuplets born in the United States in 2003 (latest data available).

• • •

If you have twins and live in Massachusetts or Connecticut, you are not alone! These states have a 25% higher rate of twin births as compared to the national average. States with the highest rate (two times the national average) of triplet births are Nebraska and New Jersey. If you live in New Mexico, Idaho, Utah, Montana, Wyoming or Hawaii, you might find it interesting to learn that these states have the lowest multiples birth rates. *NOTE: The number of fertility clinics in these areas has a large impact on the results. Did you know that there are more than 400 fertility centers in the United States? Most of them are in the Northeast.*

• • •

Expect to gain about 40–50 pounds if you are expecting twins, and about 50–60 if you are expecting triplets. Note that these are all statistical averages, and that they are significantly more than the average weight gain for singleton pregnancies (25–35 pounds). Don't be surprised if your weight gain does not fall into these ranges. For comparison purposes, I gained 72 pounds with my triplets (I delivered at 33+ weeks, and they all weighed just over 4 pounds each). I also know a woman who gained a whopping 102 pounds with her triplets, and another who had twins and gained only 19 pounds (with each baby weighing over 6 pounds at birth). Talk to your doctor if you have any concerns about your weight gain, or lack of it. *NOTE: The average birth weight for a singleton is 7½ pounds, which is significantly more than twins (5½ pounds) and triplets (3¾ pounds).*

• • •

Stork Net's Pregnancy Week-by-Week Guide *(www.pregnancyguide online.com)* is a great place to track "average" week-by-week growth. If you click on specific weeks, it will give you helpful information and tips specific to multiple gestation. It's not very detailed, but interesting! Did you know that (according to the American Pregnancy Association), twins typically grow at the same rate as singletons, up to about week 30? Triplets also grow at the same rate as singletons up to 26–27 weeks. At this point, they gain weight at a slower rate than singletons. Thank goodness! Can you imagine the enormity of your belly if they didn't? *NOTE: Expectant mothers of twins' bellies are about 6–8 weeks larger than women carrying singletons, and women having triplets are usually*

10–12 weeks larger. In other words, at 6 months gestation, expectant mothers of twins look like they are 8 months pregnant, and those with triplets look full term!

• • •

The chart that follows shows the results of a study that tracked fetal weights for singletons versus twins and triplets. According to the summary, it looks as if the decline in weight in multiple gestation in this study actually began sooner (19 weeks for triplets, and about 25 weeks for twins) than the American Pregnancy Association suggests, although there is nothing of significance until the weeks they described.

Fetal Age (in weeks)	Average Fetal Weight		
	Singleton	Twin	Triplet
16	2.2 oz	2.5 oz	3.1 oz
17	4.6 oz	4.8 oz	5.2 oz
18	7.1 oz	7.3 oz	7.4 oz
19	9.8 oz	9.9 oz	9.7 oz
20	12.7 oz	12.9 oz	12.3 oz
21	15.9 oz	15.9 oz	15.1 oz
22	1 lb 3 oz	1 lb 3 oz	1 lb 2 oz
23	1 lb 6 oz	1 lb 6 oz	1 lb 5 oz
24	1 lb 10 oz	1 lb 10 oz	1 lb 8 oz
25	1 lb 15 oz	1 lb 14 oz	1 lb 12 oz
26	2 lbs 3 oz	2 lbs 2 oz	2 lbs
27	2 lbs 8 oz	2 lbs 6 oz	2 lbs 4 oz
28	2 lbs 12 oz	2 lbs 10 oz	2 lbs 8 oz
29	3 lbs 1 oz	2 lbs 15 oz	2 lbs 13 oz
30	3 lbs 6 oz	3 lbs 4 oz	3 lbs 1 oz
31	3 lbs 12 oz	3 lbs 9 oz	3 lbs 6 oz
32	4 lbs 2 oz	3 lbs 14 oz	3 lbs 11 oz
33	4 lbs 8 oz	4 lbs 3 oz	4 lbs
34	4 lbs 15 oz	4 lbs 9 oz	4 lbs 6 oz
35	5 lbs 5 oz	4 lbs 15 oz	4 lbs 12 oz
36	5 lbs 12 oz	5 lbs 5 oz	5 lbs 3 oz
37	6 lbs 4 oz	5 lbs 11 oz	–
38	6 lbs 11oz	6 lbs 2 oz	–
39	7 lbs 3 oz	6 lbs 9 oz	–
40	7 lbs 11 oz	7 lbs	–

Keep in mind that this information is approximate. Each pregnancy is different and growth rates vary. Source: The Oxford Journals

• • •

To get a visual idea of what your babies might look like each week, go to *http://pregnancy.about.com/od/multiplepregnancy/a/multiplesus.htm*

to see multiple gestation sonogram photos by week. There are twins, a few triplets, and even quadruplets! If you would like to get an idea of what you might look like along the way, check out the "multiples belly gallery" at *http://pregnancy.about.com/od/multiplepregnancy/ig/ Multiple-Pregnancy-Gallery/index.htm.*

• • •

Consider taking a "multiples" baby care class. Many also offer child safety as part of the course. Visit *www.marvelousmultiples.com* to find a multiples prenatal education class near you. Most classes are hospital based and are open to anyone expecting twins or more. No matter what baby care class you sign up for, be sure to enroll early (ideally between 15 and 20 weeks gestation). *NOTE: If you can't find a multiples baby care class in your area, or if you end up on bedrest, you can learn from a DVD instead. "Expecting Multiples" does a good job educating parents in the comfort of their own homes. You can order the DVD ($39.95) online at* www.expectingmultiples.com.

• • •

Get your hands on as much information as you can regarding nutrition for multiple pregnancies, and eat as healthy as possible. You will need to put on more weight and will need to gain it sooner than you might think. Early weight gain in expectant mothers of twins or more is critically important, because every ounce of weight a mother gains will help her babies (especially if she gives birth very prematurely). The Triplet Connection *(www.tripletconnection.org)* is an excellent source for nutrition information, as well as Dr. Barbara Luke's website *(www.drbarbaraluke.com)*. For $50, Dr. Luke (the author of *When You are Expecting Twins, Triplets or Quads*) will give you a complete dietary evaluation. Marvelous Multiples *(www.marvelousmultiples.com)* also offers a nutrition guide — *Nourishing Marvelous Multiples* ($7.95). In addition, don't forget to ask your doctor for information.

• • •

As you might expect, nausea is more common and often worse for those expecting more than one baby. If you experience this, carry large resealable plastic bags with you. Keep a few next to your bed, in your purse, in your desk at work, and in your car. You never know when one might come in handy!

• • •

The following are some Mom-to-be suggestions that may help reduce your feelings of nausea:

- Try to eat six to eight small meals a day, rather than three large ones.
- Put a few drops of lemon juice on a handkerchief and carry it with you. If a smell bothers you, cover your nose with the handkerchief.
- Carry a box of scented soap in your purse. Smelling a fresh scent can mask certain odors that may turn your stomach.
- Carry bland crackers and snack on them throughout the day.
- Keep crackers in your nightstand and eat a few before getting out of bed.
- Avoid fatty or fried foods.
- Avoid rich, acidic, and spicy foods.
- Drink ginger ale or ginger tea.
- Try acupressure wristbands (typically used for seasickness).
- Talk to your doctor about adding or eliminating certain vitamins in your diet.
- If you suffer from severe nausea, ask your doctor about alternatives, including medication.

• • •

Drink *lots* of water, and get into the habit of taking liquids with you everywhere you go. Plenty of hydration is especially important because it helps to stop the risk of premature uterine contractions and early delivery. *NOTE: Ask your doctor how much you should be drinking on a daily basis.*

• • •

Buy a small organizer/notebook to keep track of doctor's appointments, baby shower ideas, thoughts for baby names, nursery ideas, general to-dos, and other important notes. Carry it with you and jot down your thoughts as they come to you.

• • •

As questions about your pregnancy arise, write them down and take your list of questions with you to your doctor's appointments. Be sure to ask all your questions regarding your pregnancy. One of the worst things you can do is feel as if you are asking a "dumb" question. Your doctor gets paid to answer questions. Make sure your doctor answers *all* of yours!

•••

Whenever possible, ask your spouse or someone else you also feel comfortable with to accompany you to your appointments to help ensure that nothing is misinterpreted or forgotten. This person does not have to be in the room with you while you are being examined, just there for discussions with your doctor.

•••

If you have a cell phone, carry it with you at all times. It's also a good idea to keep a few important numbers in your wallet, as well as programmed into your phone. These should include your doctor, your spouse's cell and work numbers, and your boss (if you so desire). If you have other young children, carry phone numbers for at least two local people you can call to care for them in the event of an emergency, or a longer-than-expected doctor's visit.

•••

As much as you might not like the idea while you are expecting, consider taking a picture of your belly profile to capture your month-by-month growth. You will quickly forget what you looked like, unless you have pictures. Take one last picture before you leave for the hospital. It can be amusing (especially for your children) to look back at them.

•••

Save money on maternity clothing by digging into your husband's closet. Use his t-shirts and other oversized clothing instead of spending a small fortune on clothes you won't be wearing for more than a few months. Also note that you probably won't be venturing out of your home much once you start lumbering instead of walking, or you may find yourself on bedrest and won't have a need for many outfits.

•••

As your body grows, use a "body pillow" for more comfort as you sleep or just try to relax and get comfortable. Body pillows are long, oversized pillows you can find in just about any store that sells bed linens and pillows. When you buy one, make sure your spouse doesn't steal it (they are known for this). If he does, at least this will take the mystery out of what to get him for his birthday!

• • •

Don't be the only informed one on the subject of multiples. Encourage your spouse, grandparents, and anyone else who may be playing a role in caring for your children. When you read, choose your topics carefully. Focus on the positives and live by them. *NOTE: Dads can visit* www.multidad.com *("Where everyone knows how sleep deprived you are") and the "father's forum" on the Triplet Connection's website* (www.tripletconnection.org). *Grandparents can visit the "grandparents" message board at* www.twinsmagazine.com.

• • •

Get a "visual" idea of what to expect. Find a mom in your area with infant multiples, and ask if you can come for a brief visit. Most likely, she will be happy to have you (and may not want you to leave!). This can be quite a learning experience! Get in touch with your local multiples' club if you don't know someone to call.

• • •

Stock up on frozen dinners in advance of the birth. You won't have time to prepare much of anything for dinner the first few weeks unless you can find it in your freezer and toss it into the oven. If you manage to find the time after your babies are born, get into the habit of making double or triple batches when you cook. Stock up on take-out menus as well.

• • •

Put together a "To Do" list and hand it to your spouse! There is nothing more important than keeping your physical and mental stress levels down and focusing on what matters most — staying pregnant. In hindsight, one of the dumbest things I did while pregnant was think I could continue to do everything, and then some, because I had to prepare for triplets. I was obsessed with getting everything ready, and also continued to work my usual 50+ hours a week. It wasn't until one of my routine checkups quickly put an end to all of this. My cervix went from being long and thick one week, to short and thin the next. Luckily, this did not happen until 28 weeks, but it could have been much sooner. It is now *your* chance to relax and really take care of yourself and your babies. Just remember: You can be replaced at work, but *no one* can replace your babies!

• • •

Set short-term goals and celebrate every milestone. Most expectant mothers set weekly goals. If one week at a time is too much, take things one day at a time.

• • •

Take time to enjoy your pregnancy. It is truly is a multiple blessing, and it doesn't last as long as most. The typical twin pregnancy is 36½ weeks, and the typical triplet pregnancy is 33 weeks, which is significantly less than a singleton gestation of 40 weeks.

"I would recommend that any expectant parent read a week-by-week book about their pregnancy, as well as a book about what to expect in the first year. Although these books don't focus on multiple births, I found them to be relevant and informative."
— A quote from a mother of twins on the Internet

GAINING...SUPPORT

J oin a multiples support group while you are expecting. Don't make the mistake of waiting until you give birth. The knowledge you gain from others in these organizations is probably at its peak during this stage. You will be amazed at the number of instant friendships, common interests, great advice, and other benefits you will gain by becoming a member.

• • •

If you can't join a mothers of multiples support group while you are expecting, join one as soon as practical, even if you can only attend meetings once every few months. If you are not aware of any clubs in your area, visit the NOMOTC — National Organization of Mothers of Twins Clubs (www.nomotc.org). This organization has over 475 local clubs in its nationwide membership. They are listed by state, and have website and e-mail information for most clubs, so it's easy to find and contact a club in your area. *NOTE: There are also lots of clubs that are not part of the NOMOTC which you will probably be able to find by word-of-mouth.*

• • •

If you don't have a multiples club in your immediate area, form one! Put a notice in a local newspaper that you are organizing a group. Even if you get less than a handful of people to respond, you can start with a few members and continue to spread the word. The NOMOTC offers a booklet entitled, *How to Organize a Parent's of Multiples Club* that you can request from their executive office through their website.

• • •

Many new and expectant mothers find their family and friends to be a good support system. Even if a family member or friend may be far away, a phone conversation can make for a good sounding board. Online friends can also be very helpful. You can make new pregnant friends by visiting various message boards for additional support. Some of the more popular forums dedicated to multiples (in alphabetical order) are:

Best for twins:
Raising Multiples *(www.raisingmultiples.com)*
Twins Magazine *(www.twinsmagazine.com)*
Twin Shock *(www.twinshock.net)*
*Twin Stuff *(www.twinstuff.com)*
Twinteresting *(www.twinteresting.com)*

Best for triplets:
MOST (Mothers of Supertwins) *(www.mostonline.org)*
The Triplet Connection *(www.tripletconnection.org)*

* Did you know that Twin Stuff was created by identical twin brothers who married identical twin sisters? It's true! Craig and Mark Sanders met their wives at a Twins Days Festival in Twinsburg, Ohio. I am not sure if it was love at first (or second) sight, but they proposed at the same time, bought matching engagement rings, had a double wedding, their brides wore matching wedding gowns, they built homes next door to each other, and they even share a dog! The brothers now work together for Twinstuff Outreach, and if that wasn't enough "twin stuff," one of the couples now has a set of identical twin boys! *NOTE: The Twins Days Festival began in 1976, when a total of 37 families gathered to celebrate their special bond of "twin-ship." Over the years, the festival has grown to close*

to 3,000 twins that gather in Twinsburg, Ohio each year. To learn more about the annual Twins Days Festival, visit www.twinsdays.org. *The Triplet Connection also hosts an annual convention for families with triplets. Since there is no "Triplets-ville" to speak of, their convention site changes each year. For more information, visit* www.tripletconnection.org.

· · ·

Visit Twins Magazine *(www.twinsmagazine.com)*. This site has message boards, lots of shopping links (you can find many of the multiple-related e-tailers that sell merchandise), and a bi-monthly magazine that you can subscribe to.

· · ·

If you are expecting triplets, contact the Triplet Connection *(www.triplet connection.org)* and Mothers of Supertwins *(www.mostonline.org)* and ask for their "expectant parent" packages. These are invaluable resources for those expecting higher order multiples. If you contact the Triplet Connection, you also get a copy of their book, *Exceptional Pregnancies* as part of the package. They also have a twin's version of this book.

· · ·

The following is contact information to order magazines/newsletters dedicated to multiples. They are fun to read, and very helpful:

Twin Publications:
Twins Magazine — www.twinsmagazine.com — (888) 558-9467
Mothers of Twins Clubs Notebook — www.nomotc.org — (877) 540-2200

Triplet Publications:
Supertwins Magazine — www.mostonline.org — (631) 859-1110
The Triplet Connection — www.tripletconnection.org — (435) 851-1105

If you subscribe to any of these, do so as soon as possible, because some can take several weeks to arrive.

"My twins club really saved my life. People with older multiples have always been there, day or night, to calm me down whenever my life gets turned upside down."
— A quote from a mother in the *Home News Tribune*

DOCTORS AND HOSPITALS

I f at all possible, choose to team up with a reputable group of perinatologists (obstetricians who specialize in high-risk pregnancies for both mother and fetuses). If your doctor is an obstetrician who does not specialize in high-risk pregnancies, seriously consider one who does. For more information regarding perinatologists, visit the Society for Maternal Fetal Medicine *(www.smfm.org)*. The society offers a physician locator and can answer many of your questions about the benefits of being under the care of a perinatologist.

● ● ●

Is your obstetrician sending you to a perinatologist every month for a checkup? If so, why not use the perinatologist as your doctor? After all, you are considered a high-risk pregnancy. I was in this situation and when I made the decision to switch doctors, I was glad I did. I made my decision as a result of pressure from a pediatrician/friend of mine, and because my obstetrician told me I would be transferred to another doctor and hospital if I gave birth before 30 weeks gestation!

• • •

When I switched from a group of obstetricians to a group of perinatologists, I noted the following differences:

- There were far fewer patients in the waiting room.
- The doctor(s) had more time for me.
- Most patients were expecting twins or more.
- Appointments were longer and more frequent.
- Sonograms were more frequent and very detailed.
- They took extra precautions — more tests and monitoring.
- The doctors and nurses were more knowledgeable about nutrition.
- The doctors were able to answer all of my questions (this was not the case with my previous doctors).
- The group was affiliated with the best-equipped hospital in the area.
- They were truly multiple birth experts.

• • •

Unless you don't have a choice, make every effort to deliver your babies in a hospital that offers a Level III neonatal intensive care unit (NICU — pronounced "Nick-you"). These hospitals provide the most advanced care, and are the best equipped to care for premature or sick infants. Level III hospitals also have neonatologists on staff at all times and are ready for any emergency. Neonatologists are specialists trained to handle the most complex, high-risk situations, and use equipment that is specially designed for the tiniest of patients. *NOTE: There are also a handful of Level IV NICUs in the United States. Your doctor should be able to tell you if there are any in your area.*

• • •

According to *Parents Magazine,* about 20% of twins and 80% of triplets go to intensive care following their birth, and according to the American College of Obstetricians & Gynecologists, the average hospital stay for twins is 18 days (typically ranging from 9–25 days); and triplets 30 days (typically ranging from 11–90 days). Make every effort to find the best hospital for your babies — the facility where they are born *really* makes a difference!

• • •

I recently read a story in my local newspaper headlined, "Surprise!" It was a story about a couple who were expecting twins, until late in the pregnancy when they discovered triplets were on the way. The triplets were born in the hospital their obstetrician typically delivered in, and the article said, "It was the third set of triplets born (in that hospital) in more than seven years." My thoughts after reading this story were: 1) If the mother had worked with a perinatologist, she would have known about her triplets much sooner; 2) With a perinatologist, she would have delivered in a Level III hospital about 10 minutes from the one she delivered in (the hospital I am referring to has delivered more than 140 sets of triplets in the past seven years); and 3) What would she have done if she delivered at 30 weeks instead of 35? Think about what you would do if you found yourself in this situation. *NOTE: About 35% of twins and 85% of triplets are born before 35 weeks gestation.*

• • •

If you plan to deliver in a Level III (or IV) hospital, call and ask if you can take a tour of its NICU to help you prepare for the very real possibility of premature birth. When you go, don't view the NICU as intimidating; instead, remember that the smallest of premature babies have the best chance of survival in these facilities. *NOTE: Babies born at 28 weeks now have a greater than 90% chance of survival in these facilities. ANOTHER NOTE: Some hospitals may not allow tours of their facility in an effort to keep germs and disturbances out.*

• • •

Make it a priority and become familiar with the quickest route to the hospital. Remember that the shortest route isn't necessarily the quickest route. Do this well in advance of your due date. Also, make sure you always have gas in your tank, especially in the third trimester. You won't want to get halfway to the hospital and have to power-walk the rest of the way!

THE NAME GAME

f you *ask* family and friends for help in naming your babies, don't be surprised by some of the silly suggestions they come up with! They won't be able to resist, because it's all part of the novelty and fun that comes with the territory. You may hear, "Why don't you name them 'Bert & Ernie,' like those two guys from Sesame Street?" or "What about 'Frick & Frack'?" If you need names for triplets, someone might suggest, "How about Larry, Moe and Curly?" Although everyone is bound to get a few laughs during the process, finding names for your children may be tougher than you'd expect! Consider the following:

1) There are lots of interesting ways to choose names for multiples, other than simply picking from a list of names in a baby book.

2) There's a chance you might like the idea of similar names initially, and later change your mind, or vice-versa.

3) It may be more difficult to talk your spouse into two (or three) names that you have your heart set on (versus the usual amount of coaxing needed for one).

4) Deciding on one name is tough enough, never mind two or three!

5) If you don't want to know the sexes, you will need four names for twins and six for triplets — agreeing on this many names could take longer than the pregnancy!

NOTE: Did you know that "Frick & Frack" were not twins, but stage names for two Swiss comedy ice skaters? They came to the U.S. and joined the original Ice Follies show which began in 1936 and ran for almost 50 years. Larry, Moe and Curly (also known as the "Three Stooges") were an American comedy slapstick act in the 20th century.

• • •

Some parents of multiples prefer names that are "related" in some way, other than names that are "related" simply because they sound alike. Here are some name associations (and examples) to think about if you have any interest in doing this:

- Rhyming or similar sounding (Brenna & Jenna)
- Same beginning (Mason, Macy & Mack)
- Same ending (Caroline & Madeline)
- Same beginning and ending (Brooklyn & Bradyn)
- Sequential letters of the alphabet (Alexander, Blake and Carter)
- Similar meaning (Hunter, Trapper & Tanner)
- Unisex (Taylor & Jordan)
- Male/Female version of same name (Michael & Micheala)
- Names in reverse (Noel & Leon)
- Celebrity names (Jada & Jewel)
- TV characters (Bree, Edie & Gabrielle)
- Sports figures (Peyton & Eli)

- Most popular names in their birth year (Matthew & Madison)
- Traditional (Jennifer & Michael)
- Trendy/Modern (Jaz & Jett)
- Similarly unusual (Skandar & Sennett)
- Family names (Carson & Parker)
- Grandparents names (Gus & Ella)
- Same ethnic background (Conor, Aidan & Riley)
- Names of places (Kenya & Dakota)
- Names of cities (Savannah & Austin)
- Names associated with a season (Summer & August)
- Heavenly names (Christian, Trinity & Genesis)
- Completely different names (Jane & Zipporah)
- Same length (Ben, Max, & Sam)
- Same middle name (Lauren Anne & Mary Anne)
- Names with the same initials (BAL/BAL)
- Deciding on names simply because you like them
- Come up with your own "related" names — the possibilities are endless!

Another unconventional (to say the least) alternative: Consider naming both/all of your children after yourself, like George Foremen (two-time world boxing champion) did. George Foreman has ten children (5 boys/ 5 girls) and has named all of his sons "George Edward Foreman" and one of his daughters "Georgetta." George chose to do this because his biological father never took part in his upbringing, and he "wants his children to know who their father is." I guess this makes sense, but I still can't figure out why he also named a grill after himself. Can you? Marketing ingenuity?

...

If you plan to do your name searching online, it might be helpful to visit some of the more popular baby name sites. These include (but are not limited to):

www.babynames.com
www.parentsplace.com
www.parentsoup.com

www.babynamesworld.com
www.babyzone.com
www.babycenter.com

• • •

The following "names" web pages may be lengthy to type, but are well worth taking a look at because they relate specifically to twins (or triplets):

1) *http://en.wikipedia.org/wiki/List_of_twins* — (historical twins, twin celebrities, twins in sports, famous twins and more)

2) *http://en.wikipedia.org/wiki/List_of_twins_in_fiction* — (twins in fiction)

3) *http://www.lowchensaustralia.com/names/twinnames.htm* — (names of famous "duos")

4) *http://www.anagramgenius.com/twins.html* — (anagrams for twins, triplets)

5) *http://www.behindthename.com* — (list of logical names for twins — many are unusual)

6) *http://www.socialsecurity.gov/OACT/babynames/twins.html* — (top twin names)

• • •

Be sure to take a look at the U.S. Social Security Administration's website *(www.socialsecurity.gov/OACT/babynames/twins.html)*. Among lots of other information, this is what I found:

MOST POPULAR NAMES FOR TWINS
Latest data available (based on Social Security card applications)
Source: U.S. Social Security Administration

1 Jacob, Joshua	34 Faith, Grace	67 Megan, Morgan
2 Matthew, Michael	35 Jacob, Jordan	68 Samuel, Sophia
3 Daniel, David	36 Jacob, Matthew	69 Aidan, Ava
4 Faith, Hope	37 Jaden, Jordan	70 Alexander, Alexis
5 Ethan, Evan	38 Alexander, Anthony	71 Andrew, Anthony
6 Taylor, Tyle	39 Brandon, Bryan	72 Andrew, Ethan
7 Isaac, Isaiah	40 Emily, Sarah	73 Andrew, William
8 Joseph, Joshua	41 Ethan, Nathan	74 Ava, Olivia
9 Nathan, Nicholas	42 Jacob, Joseph	75 Caleb, Jacob
10 Madison, Mason	43 Jordan, Joshua	76 Jacob, Nicholas
11 Hailey, Hannah	44 Landon, Logan	77 Jacob, Ryan
12 Madison, Morgan	45 Olivia, Sophia	78 Jake, Luke
13 Alexander, Andrew	46 Ashley, Emily	79 Jayden, Jordan
14 Elijah, Isaiah	47 Elizabeth, Emily	80 John, William
15 Jordan, Justin	48 Elizabeth, Katherine	81 Mark, Matthew
16 Mackenzie, Madison	49 Jeremy, Joshua	82 Natalie, Nathan
17 Alexander, Nicholas	50 John, Joseph	83 Nathaniel, Nicholas
18 Caleb, Joshua	51 Nathan, Noah	84 Ryan, Tyler
19 Emma, Ethan	52 Nicholas, Noah	85 Abigail, Emily
20 Jonathan, Joshua	53 Nicholas, Zachary	86 Anna, Emma
21 Emily, Ethan	54 Alexander, Christopher	87 Anthony, Michael
22 Alexander, Benjamin	55 Christopher, Michael	88 Anthony, Nicholas
23 Andrew, Matthew	56 Jacob, Zachary	89 Austin, Justin
24 Benjamin, Samuel	57 Jason, Justin	90 Benjamin, Jacob
25 James, John	58 Abigail, Allison	91 Brian, Brianna
26 Matthew, Nicholas	59 Amy, Emily	92 Christopher, Matthew
27 Brandon, Brian	60 Andrew, Nicholas	93 Daniel, Samuel
28 Ella, Emma	61 Benjamin, William	94 Gabriel, Michael
29 Alexander, Zachary	62 Christopher, Nicholas	95 Haley, Hannah
30 Dylan, Tyler	63 Ella, Ethan	96 Jada, Jaden
31 Hannah, Sarah	64 Gabriella, Isabella	97 Jayden, Jaylen
32 Madison, Matthew	65 Isabella, Sophia	98 Jonathan, Joseph
33 Christian, Christopher	66 Jeremiah, Joshua	99 Kyle, Ryan
		100 Logan, Lucas

Here is a quick summary of the "Top 10 Names for Twins" by gender:

BOYS	GIRLS	BOY/GIRL
1 Jacob, Joshua	1 Faith, Hope	1 Taylor, Tyler
2 Matthew, Michael	2 Hailey, Hannah	2 Madison, Mason
3 Daniel, David	3 Madison, Morgan	3 Emma, Ethan
4 Ethan, Evan	4 Mackenzie, Madison	4 Emily, Ethan
5 Isaac, Isaiah	5 Ella, Emma	5 Madison, Matthew
6 Joseph, Joshua	6 Hannah, Sarah	6 Jaden, Jordan
7 Nathan, Nicholas	7 Faith, Grace	7 Ella, Ethan
8 Alexander, Andrew	8 Emily, Sarah	8 Sophia, Samuel
9 Elijah, Isaiah	9 Olivia, Sophia	9 Ava, Aiden
10 Jordan, Justin	10 Ashley, Emily	10 Alexis, Alexander

• • •

The following is a list of web pages to take a look at while you are on the U.S. Social Security Administration's (SSA) website in search of baby names:

1) To see a listing of the latest "top 100" twin names available, go to *www.socialsecurity.gov/OACT/babynames/twins.html*

2) To see a listing of most popular singleton names for the most current year, visit *www.socialsecurity.gov/OACT/babynames/*

3) This site also has most popular singleton names dating as far back as 1880! If you go to *www.socialsecurity.gov/OACT/babynames/* and scroll down to the bottom of the page, you will see a section called "Popular Names by Birth Year." Type in any birth year dating as far back as 1880, and see a list of the most popular 1,000 names for that year! When I searched for the most popular names in 1880, I found "Buford" and "Bertha" on the list, and I also found "Hunter" and "Hannah," which are very popular names today!

4) Just to the left of that same web page, *www.socialsecurity. gov/OACT/babynames/*, is a section where you can look up "Popular Names by State." This will give you a listing of names dating as far back as 1960.

5) If you are not sure where to find this information on the Social Security Administration's website, go to the main site, *www.socialsecurity.gov,* and do a search for the information you are looking for.

• • •

For those of you expecting triplets, I was not able to find any information on the SSA's website for triplet names. However, if you have your heart set on finding popular names for your babies, the twin lists should be helpful, and so should the singleton lists of names dating back to 1880. Another place to look for triplet names is in the back of the Triplet Connection magazine. Each issue announces the birth of members' newborn triplets.

• • •

Speaking of triplet names…did you know a woman from Virginia apparently put the naming rights to her triplets up for auction on eBay? *GoldenPalace.com* used the "buy now" option to buy the rights for $12,000! A spokesperson for the company said one of the babies will be named "GoldenPalace.com." The other two names will be revealed when the babies are born. YIKES! This is probably not the best way to go about naming your triplets! *NOTE:* GoldenPalace.com *is an online casino well-known for its outlandish publicity stunts.*

• • •

Similar names are no doubt nice for multiples. In fact, about 30% of new parents of multiples give their children similar sounding names, and about 15% choose names that start with the same letter. If you are thinking of doing this, just realize that similar names may add to the confusion that already comes with the territory, especially if your multiples are identical. I found that many people who knew us, and knew us well, confused me with my twin because we had similar names (Lisa and Lynn). I often thought if our names were very different (but perhaps related in a different way, other than the same length and same first letter), people would not have fumbled with our names as often as they did. It was very common to hear someone say, "Lisa, I mean Lynn" whenever they called me by name. This happened all the time and I honestly believe people confused the names with the faces, more so than they confused the faces with the names. I also know a set of triplets who share the same first letter of their names. Although I know them by looks, I often take roll call before I get their names straight. *NOTE: I am by no means suggesting that you should not choose similar names for your children. My mother did, and so do many others! Just be sure to consider the consequences and accept them before making any decisions about what to name your children.*

• • •

If you choose names with a different first letter, you can use their initials to identify bottles, shoes, clothing, and other things. Once you have decided on names, just be careful the initials don't spell something embarrassing!

• • •

If you are concerned about individuality, try to avoid names that suggest your multiples are part of a set (i.e. Paula and Paulette). Distinctly different names will help them to feel like individuals. On the other hand, if you would prefer that they feel like a pair (or group), consider similar names for your children.

• • •

It may be wise to avoid names that are difficult to remember or pronounce. Since these names can be a challenge to begin with, imagine how difficult it might be to remember two or three of them. Also, if you try to be too cute, you might regret it. I once met a girl named *April May June*. Imagine triplet girls with these names? I can't, but can only imagine the fun others might have at their expense! *NOTE: Donald Duck's nieces were also April, May and June. I wonder if April May June's parents were big Donald Duck fans?*

• • •

After you give birth, sound out your babies' names in their birth order and make sure you like the way it sounds before signing any documents. If you are like most parents, you will probably find yourself referring to your kids in their birth order, and you will likely refer to them as a pair (or group) much more than you will on an individual basis. If you sound out the names in their birth order and it turns into a tongue twister or just sounds odd, you might want to switch names around (unless you hesitate to give your daughter the name that was intended for your son, and vice-versa)!

• • •

Don't forget that the names you choose will be something you will have to live with the rest of your life, and so will your children. So, take your time and find names that you love!

THINGS YOU'D RATHER AVOID
BUT CAN'T

Talk about who the guardians will be for your children should something happen to you and your spouse. Making this decision is difficult enough with one child, and it is even more complex with multiples (i.e., Would you prefer to keep them together or separate them? Does it make more sense to keep your children together for their emotional well-being? If so, will the guardian you choose be in a position to care for more than one child? Is the guardian willing and committed to caring for more than one child?). Work through these issues, talk with potential guardians and as soon as you make your decisions, meet with an attorney who specializes in estates and wills. Put your intentions in writing and once you do, you will sleep better at night.

• • •

Many parents think they don't need a will because they don't have large estates. This is not true! A will is essential if you have children. If you and your spouse die without a will, a court will appoint guardians for your children.

• • •

Yesterday was the best time to make sure you have adequate life insurance. Make this your number one priority, and take time to talk to a trusted financial advisor about the best options for your family. Also, don't forget to think about insurance for a stay-at-home parent. If this person dies prematurely, will your family be able to replace the daily contributions this person makes to your family? This has a real economic value: Make sure you protect it with adequate life insurance.

• • •

Disability insurance will be just as important as life insurance, especially if one spouse works to support your family. About 80% of the time, misfortunes in families do not result in death, but rather a disability. When a primary breadwinner becomes disabled and is no longer able to work, many families end up in dire financial straits as a result of inadequate or lack of disability insurance. Keep this in mind when shopping for insurance.

WORKING OUT WORK-RELATED ISSUES

I f you are employed, find out about every benefit your company offers expectant mothers and fathers (your spouse should do the same). Get in touch with your companies' medical and human resource departments (if you have them) and ask lots of questions. Many companies have benefits you may not be aware of, including car seat programs, special offers on breast pumps, affiliations with certain daycare centers, and more. You might be surprised to find how accommodating your company is with regard to your pregnancy.

• • •

Ask your human resource department about maternity benefits in general. Also, if you plan to return to work, ask the following questions:

- How many weeks will the company pay in full while you are on maternity leave?
- Does your company offer extended leave? If so, what are your options?

- Will you have your current position when you return?
- What will happen if you are put on bedrest for any length of time?
- Think of other things that may be important to you and find out what your company's policy is.

• • •

Don't make any "official" decisions about returning to work until the *end* of your maternity leave. If you decide to give your boss time to find your replacement, don't be surprised if your company revokes all of the benefits you would have been entitled to. Make sure you get paid and keep your health insurance and disability benefits. Something else to consider: You might change your mind about returning to work after the babies are born.

• • •

If you think you might want to return to work on a part-time basis, inquire about it as soon as possible. Don't wait until your water breaks and expect your company to offer you a part-time position! Give your boss enough time to work out a plan. If you ask up front and your boss tells you to go jump in a lake, at least you will have given yourself time to dry off, swallow your pride, and work on other options and opportunities.

• • •

If you are planning to return to work on a part-time basis, it might make sense to prepare to go back within the usual six to eight weeks after you deliver. If you want your company to consider a part-time position for you, offer something in return and use it as a bargaining chip. Don't expect to take six months off and then return on a part-time basis. Your boss might not be receptive to your plan.

• • •

If you plan to go back to work on a full-time basis, whether it be for financial reasons or the coffee and lunch breaks, think about asking for the maximum time your company will allow for maternity leave. Some larger companies will keep your job for up to six months or guarantee a job after extended leave for up to one year (although it may not be the job you left). If you can afford to do this, realize a multiple birth is a perfect reason to ask for additional time off.

• • •

Do you plan to return to work and make immediate use of a daycare facility? If so, sign your unborn children up as soon as possible. The sooner you get on the enrollment list, the better, even if it's several months before your due date. Enrolling in some daycare facilities can be like applying to any Ivy League college! There may be tests, interviews, applications, pulling a few strings, and praying for a miracle that you get in. Since you will need two or three applications, it's almost a sure bet that there may not be availability when you need it. So, think smart and plan ahead!

• • •

Many larger companies have on-site childcare, which offers an added convenience for employees. If your company has a facility, realize that it is perfectly fine to get on the enrollment list without announcing your pregnancy at work (unless the daycare director is married to your boss!). Daycare facilities are often managed by organizations separate from the company that uses it.

• • •

If you plan to return to work shortly after your maternity leave, consider a childcare provider that cares for your children in your home while they are infants. Packing yourself, your babies, and all the gear that gets hauled along with them to a daycare center can prove to be very difficult and expensive. With multiples, you will probably find it much more convenient to have care in your home at this stage.

• • •

Consider childcare outside of your home when your children approach the toddler stage (two+ years). At this point, the benefits outweigh the inconveniences. As toddlers, you will no longer need to carry your babies, and at this point they will benefit from a more structured, social environment.

• • •

Mull over other choices before you plan to work from home while a babysitter cares for your children in the next room. Unless your house is palatial and you can escape to one of its wings to get some work done, this can be stressful and counterproductive. Your children will have a natural desire to be with you, and telling them "no" while you work in another room will be much easier said than done, although this will not be the case while they are newborns.

• • •

Once the dust settles, you may want to consider a part-time job that allows for flexibility. Many mothers of multiples work as part-time sales representatives for companies, including Longaberger, Southern Living at Home, Pampered Chef, Avon, and others. Mothers who do this seem to really enjoy it, finding it a convenient and rewarding way to earn extra money.

• • •

If you need a job but wonder how you will manage to earn enough to cover daycare expenses, or if you have ever envisioned yourself as a business executive in a pony tail and sweatpants, visit 2Work-at-Home *(www.2work-at-home.com)* and the Home Job Stop *(www.homejobstop. com)*. Both can help you find at-home employment. These websites are dedicated to helping mothers find *paid* work-at-home careers (in addition to the at-home jobs they already have!).

• • •

If you have always dreamed about being an entrepreneur (or haven't given it any thought until now), take a look at the following websites recommended by Parents.com: *www.bizymoms.com* and *www. mompreneursonline.com.* These sites have ideas for starting your own business, including e-books and step-by-step directions on how to get started. They also have chat rooms that allow you to communicate with others involved in similar endeavors.

"My company had no corporate policy on job-sharing. All I had to do was sell my idea, and the Vice President agreed! Any mother who has an interest in working part-time owes it to herself to inquire about it, whether a policy or position exists, or not."
— Laura C. (Job-sharing Corporate Financial Controller and mother of three)

"My days at work are my days off."
— Words from several mothers of multiples who work outside their homes

---

TIME FOR BED-REST?

Ninety-nine bottles of beer on the wall, 99 bottles of beer, take one down, pass it around, 98 bottles of beer on the wall, 98 bottles of beer on the wall, 98 bottles of b-e-e-e-r, take one down, pass it around, and go stir crazy! Sounds ridiculous, but unless you are actually in this situation, you will have no way of preparing for just how boring bedrest can be! Bedrest is not something to look forward to, but must be taken very seriously, whether it lasts for a few days or a number of months.

• • •

Nap if you're tired, eat when you're hungry, eat when you're not hungry, call a friend, click on the television (if you can find the remote *and* figure out how to use it), thumb through your favorite magazine, or read a book. Now you are living — at least for a week or so, until complete boredom kicks in!

• • •

With twins or triplets on the way, there is a good chance you will end up on some form of bedrest. There are two types, and neither one of them is a bed of roses: "modified (partial)" and "strict (complete)." If your doctor prescribes either one, be sure to ask him or her to describe the specific limitations of your bedrest. "Modified" bedrest usually means spending some part of the day resting or lying down. This can mean simply "taking it easy," or staying in bed the entire day but being able to get up to shower, use the bathroom, and eat. "Strict" bedrest usually means lying down all day without getting up to do anything (and often involves the dreaded bedpan). In more extreme circumstances, strict bedrest may involve spending some time in a hospital. Be sure to fully understand and adhere to your limitations! *NOTE: Even if you don't end up on bedrest, you should rest several times a day once you reach your 20th week of pregnancy.*

• • •

Deciding where to plant your self while bedridden is another question. Unless you have no choice, look for a sunny, comfortable room, other than your bedroom, to rest in. Bedrooms can be dark and depressing if you spend an inordinate amount of time in them. If you need to transport a bed to your family room, by all means, do so (just make sure you don't move it!). Family rooms tend to be much brighter, and they are better to socialize in when you have visitors.

• • •

Consider renting a hospital bed if your bedrest is expected to last a month or more. Look up "hospital supplies" in your local phone book. Hospital beds are more comfortable than flat beds or couches if lying on them for weeks on end. They also come with controls to elevate your head and legs. You will be amazed at the added comfort and entertainment value these beds have!

• • •

If you rent a hospital bed, be sure to ask for an adjustable table to go along with it. If you don't rent a bed, use your ironing board as a table and adjust it to a comfortable height. Use it for dining and as a desk, and hold off on the ironing for a while.

• • •

If your doctor permits, take a few minutes every day to take a quick shower and get dressed. Once dressed, open the blinds and let the sun shine in! Doing this may make you feel much better as you rest.

• • •

Do you still have your college dorm refrigerator? If so, put it to good use. Place it next to your bed or couch and ask your husband to stock it with delicious, nutritious food that you can munch on throughout the day. If you can't find a small refrigerator, a cooler will suffice.

• • •

Keep a warm washcloth, napkins, paper plates, plastic utensils and a wastebasket for effortless cleanups when you eat. Put your drinks in plastic water bottles (with sipper tops) to avoid spills. The paper products you buy will also come in handy after the birth when you don't have time to wash dishes, so stock up.

• • •

Find a bookshelf, or something with shelves, and put it nearby. This will allow you to organize things you want to attend to while you have nothing better to do! Some things to place on your bookshelf might be all your TV remotes, a radio, mountains of mail, a manicure set, puzzles, a deck of cards (it's safe to assume you will be playing "solitaire" most days), games-for-one (if you can find any), photo albums that need work, needlepoint, magazines, catalogs, books, note pads, stationery, a hairbrush, and anything else that might help pass the time.

• • •

Make new friendships (or just compare beds sores) with other expectant mothers on bedrest by visiting *www.pregnancy.about.com/library/ blbedrestbuddies.htm.* Or, if you would prefer to read about other's experiences and survival tactics, go to *www.twinslist.org/bedrest.htm.*

• • •

Keep a phone within reach so you won't have to get up when it rings, and turn off the ringer when you want to rest. Keep your personal address book next to it, or program numbers into your cell phone if you plan to use it.

• • •

Speaking of phones, bedrest can be the perfect setting to run up a huge phone bill. You will find that bedrest is a great way to catch up with friends you haven't spoken to in a while and probably won't get to chat much with once your babies are born. This, coupled with boredom, can become very expensive! Be aware of this and think about continuing your conversations through e-mail.

• • •

If you have numerous calls to make but don't want to spend the money, consider using your cell phone. Review your plan and make use of as many free minutes as your service allows before picking up your house phone. Another alternative would be to sign up for a flat monthly rate. Yet another idea: Send out a mass e-mail to all of your friends and family members and inform them of your bedrest. Include your phone number and wait for them to call you!

• • •

Just yesterday I read "Real Fact # 75" under a Snapple iced tea bottle cap which read, "The average person makes about 1,140 telephone calls each year." What it forgot to mention was, "…unless you are on bedrest, in which case you will make about 1,140 calls in one month!" Keep your calls to a minimum if you need your dimes for other things.

• • •

Seek help and accept it willingly if it is offered. Ask friends and family to run errands, cook meals, and rely on them for childcare (or hire a babysitter if necessary). Once you've (literally) exhausted your resources, get in touch with a mothers of multiples club in your area. Many clubs offer meals-on-wheels, and most members will be happy to help you in any way they can. *NOTE: Buy a baby monitor in advance and put it to good use. Use it to call others to assist you when you need help: "Uh, honey, can you come into the family room? I just lost half the sandwich you made for me. It's somewhere in the couch, but I can't see over my stomach to find it. Will you please help me? I need to find it because I'm starving!"*

• • •

When the going gets tough, realize that you won't be able to lounge around like this again for another 18 years, so enjoy every monotonous moment of it!

IN-ACTIVITIES

f you don't have a laptop computer, try to borrow one. Go online, and before you know it, your bedrest days will be history! Having a laptop computer will not only help to pass the time, it can also be a great tool for obtaining lots of pertinent information while you are immobile.

• • •

Consider working at home (from your bed) to keep yourself busy. This may be the perfect way to get hold of a laptop computer and earn some money while you're at it. If you do this, be aware of the hours you are putting in. Sometimes a workday can last all day and night when there is nothing else to do. Remember to find the time to rest and relax if you plan to work from your bed.

• • •

Visit Sidelines (*www.sidelines.org*). Sidelines is an organization that provides support and advice for expectant mothers on bedrest. When you get to the site, you will find books that they recommend, including *The Pregnancy Bedrest Book: A Survival Guide for Expectant Mothers and Their Families* by Amy E. Tracey. You can also read related articles by this author that have been published by *Twins Magazine* by going to the author's website, *www.pregnancybedrest.com*.

· · ·

Get your fill of books about parenting multiples, but try to avoid "multiple-pregnancy" overload. You will soon have a jammed-packed lifetime of parenting. Take time during your pregnancy to read books you enjoy that are light and easy to read (or thick and confusing, whichever you prefer). There will be many days in your future when you wish you had more time for these books.

· · ·

Compile a phone list of those you plan to call from the hospital, and update your e-mail addresses for those you want to contact electronically. Set the addresses up in advance on your computer so you can simply hit the "send" button when you are ready to inform your family and friends of the blessed event.

· · ·

Update your Christmas or other holiday list, or create one. You will certainly want to show off your new bundles of joy in a greeting card! It's never too early to start preparing for the holidays.

· · ·

Put together a birth announcement list. Once you've completed your list, go shopping online and bookmark websites that interest you. If you decide to buy anything, order the envelopes in advance, and as soon as they arrive in the mail, start addressing them and *don't stop!* If you wait until after your babies are born, it will take you an eternity to get your announcements in the mail. Well, at least it took me an eternity!

· · ·

Shop online in advance for thank you cards so you have them on hand (and can start thanking people) as soon as the gifts start rolling in. To save time, you might also want to order a return address stamp or buy address labels. *NOTE: Family Labels* (www.familylabels.com) *has cute customized address labels. (Retail price: $24.95+)*

• • •

Update your family tree. Baby memory books always ask for this information. Find out full names, birth dates and birthplaces of your babies' siblings and parents (these should be easy), grandparents, great-grandparents, aunts, uncles, and cousins. Memory books don't always ask for all of this information, but it will be nice to include. Even if you end up not using every detail, at least you will know when to call your long lost uncle to wish him a happy birthday!

• • •

Clean out a junk drawer. Going through it won't be much fun, but it will help to pass the time and make things easier to find in the future. Once clean, you may discover the drawer is a convenient place to store baby items, or a perfect place to toss more junk!

• • •

Consider writing in a journal. Many expectant mothers find journals therapeutic and a means of helping them cope with some of their innermost feelings. In the years to come, documenting your journey into motherhood will become a treasured keepsake.

• • •

Write a letter to each of your babies. Tell them how excited you are, how you are feeling, your love for them, and any other thoughts that come to mind. Put each letter in an envelope and place them in a keepsake box or baby book.

• • •

Begin bonding with your babies by listening to their heart beats at home! Just for fun, or to put your mind at ease, you can now rent (or purchase) a fetal doppler monitor. Professional grade heart monitors can be found online at *www.storkradio.com* and *www.babybeat.com*. All you need is a credit card and a prescription from your caregiver (the FDA requires that they be rented or purchased only with the authorization of a licensed caregiver). There are various models you can rent on a monthly basis for $20–$60 per month (purchase prices range from $279–599). *NOTE: Use only a professional grade fetal heart monitor. There are a few other brands for sale that are inexpensive, but consumers claim they do not work well, if at all.*

...

Visit Twins World *(www.twinsworld.com)*. This site offers fun things for multiples and their families, including contests, photos, jokes, lots of links to other websites, and more. You can also read about the Ganz twins (twin-sister media personalities) and learn more about their "Twins Restaurant" in New York City. Twins Restaurant is the only restaurant in the world staffed entirely by identical twins. The twins work at the same time in matching outfits. If one gets sick, they both stay home, and if one gets fired, they both get fired! *NOTE: For more twin/triplet facts and trivia, visit the Twins Network* (www.twinsnetwork.com) *and Three Blue Stars* (www.threebluestars.com/multiples).

...

Get your fill of "Oprah" while you still can, because your "quality time" with her will soon be limited! I will never forget the total misconception I had of what my days would be like after my triplets were born. One of them was to take a break every day to watch Oprah. HA! The reality is, I haven't watched Oprah in more than five years, and the only chance I get to see her is if I am lucky enough to catch a glimpse of her magazine on the checkout line at the grocery store. Don't expect to watch much of anything on television following the birth. Your afternoons will be filled with lots do, and watching Oprah will most likely not be one of them.

...

Listen to your doctor and your body. Do as your doctor instructs, and sleep as much as you can to help pass the time and rest your body. After all, this is essentially what bedrest is all about!

"Although I never learned how to sew a button, I taught myself how to cross-stitch baby bibs. I found a cute Noah's Ark kit at a local Michael's store that included everything I needed. It was easier than I thought, so I made TWO of them!"
— Erin C. (Mother of BG twins)

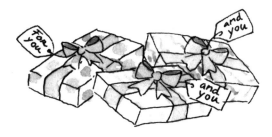

THE "BABIES" SHOWER: PLOTTING & PLANNING

Take time to register for your baby shower. Let friends and family know what you want, don't make them guess! Registering makes shopping easier for them, and makes returns easier for you.

• • •

Before you decide that "you can afford it," and choose to register (or buy) two or three of everything, realize that you won't need, nor will you want, every item for each baby. Young children have short attention spans and will get bored very quickly with a particular baby item. You will probably end up rotating your babies from one source of entertainment to another. If you have the money and desire to spend it, think about purchasing varieties of things versus feeling the need to have quantities of the same item.

...

Be *conservative* with what you think you will need. If you are not careful, your home will soon look like the inside of a self-storage facility!

...

Try to borrow as many things as you can, primarily those items you will only need for a short time. You will be amazed at how quickly your babies outgrow everything. Think of the retail value of everything you borrow as money in your pocket. You will soon be spending an unbeliev-able amount of money. Save where you can by begging and borrowing, and limit stealing to your immediate family!

...

Don't just waltz into a baby superstore one day and register. Even if you plan to spend several hours there, without planning, you may make mistakes. A first step to planning might be to visit a superstore and do nothing other than "take it all in." Spend time browsing through each aisle and jot down products that interest you (while referring to the list of suggested products in this book).

...

Do your comparison shopping online. Some of the more popular "shopping bots" include Deal Time *(www.dealtime.com)*, Price Grabber *(www.pricegrabber.com)*, Price Scan *(www.pricescan.com)*, Calibex *(www.calibex.com)*, and My Simon *(www.mysimon.com)*. These are search engines that compare prices of the same product on various web-sites. All you need to do is type in the product you are looking for, and these sites will give you the best price, and where to buy it. They will also give you a listing of different brands on the market. For example, when I went to Calibex and searched for a "baby monitor," dozens of different brands and models popped up (with photos and prices).

...

Register as soon as possible. Many expectant mothers do not register because they end up on bedrest and cannot get out to the store. Remember, you are just registering, not buying. You can shop and reg-ister online if you have to, but some stores do not offer all of their prod-ucts for sale on their websites. Also, you will probably want to test a few items and you will not be able to do this over the Internet. On the flip side, some stores have Internet exclusives, so don't forget to shop the store, as well as online. It would be a travesty to miss out on some neat new baby product!

...

Avoid registering for baby products you will not use right away. Unless you live in a home with more garages than there are people living in it, space will likely become an issue. Common mistakes parents make are registering for highchairs, wagons, gates, playpens, exersaucers, and walkers. Since you will not need these for several months (if at all), take them off your registry and think about purchasing them when the time is right.

...

Prepare to break out your credit card and purchase some larger ticket items sooner, rather than later. Necessities such as cribs, dressers, changing tables and rockers may not be in stock and could take several weeks, if not months, to be delivered (it depends on the brand). Shop for these items, decide what you would like, and as soon as you feel the time is right make your purchase.

...

Make use of the number of wheelchairs you will find in baby super-stores. They are intended for expectant mothers as well as handicapped customers.

...

Get printouts of registries from other mothers who have recently given birth to multiples. Use them as a reference guide and modify them to suit your needs.

...

When the big day arrives, you will find the term "baby shower" to be totally inappropriate for anyone expecting twins or more. A better way to describe it would be "the perfect storm." A storm of guests will arrive in droves, hauling boxes on their backs, in their arms, and some will even drag industrial strength garbage bags behind them, because they bought too many gifts and could not carry them without fear of pinching a nerve or slipping a disk. Some guests will have gifts shipped in advance, because they would rather to pay through the nose than have to lug the gifts along with them. Once all the gifts are open and the storm has passed, there will be a daunting amount of "baby stuff" scattered about, leaving the room in complete disarray. Keep this in mind, and try to avoid buying anything in advance of your shower, because you will probably get it as a gift.

. . .

Since you will be spending what will seem to be several hours opening baby gifts, be sure to take a break so your guests can get up, stretch their legs and refill their coffee cups and cake plates. Baby showers are long enough for singletons. Showers for twins or triplets often require a seventh inning stretch!

. . .

As soon as your shower is over, there is a chance you may stare in disbelief at the snow-capped mountain of gifts in front of you, and think, "Am I having a dream about working in the stock room at Babies "R" Us, or is all of this baby gear really mine?" At that moment, the "concept" of having multiples will likely become a reality, as you say to yourself, "WOW! I'm *really* having twins (triplets)! What am I going to do with all of this stuff, and better yet, what am I going to do with *two (three)* babies?" This happens to just about all of us, so be prepared!

. . .

Save those boxes and receipts! There will be shower gifts that you will need to return for one reason or another. Find a shoebox and put all the receipts in one place. Don't worry if a gift did not come with a receipt. If you end up with store credit, chances are good you will use the credit, and then some, on the same day you return the item(s).

. . .

Save all the cute baby gift bags from your shower and recycle them when it's your turn to give a baby gift. These bags are expensive and you will have a lifetime supply of them following your shower.

. . .

Expect that gifts will continue to roll in for quite some time. Keep notes of what gifts you received and from whom, and make every effort to send thank-you notes as soon as you get a chance. If you don't, you might forget to thank a few people, forget what they gave you, or won't have the time once you get caught up in other responsibilities.

THINGS TO CONSIDER/THINGS TO AVOID

When it comes to registering, the list that follows is a good start, but realize that it is not *your* list. Keep in mind that what is essential for one person could be useless to someone else. Don't buy a playpen just because a good friend told you she couldn't live without one. Does she have multiples? Is there a space issue in your home? Does your sister have one she isn't using? These are some of the questions you should ask yourself before you make any purchasing decisions.

• • •

The products I have itemized are not absolute essentials, but what I would call "conveniences." Take time to evaluate each item. Also, there are bound to be a few items that are not mentioned that you will want.

• • •

NOTE: If an item on the following list does not have "PER CHILD" next to it, the number indicated is the amount recommended for both/all your babies. If an item has a question mark (?) following it, it may not be necessary.

• • •

Clothing/Cover-ups:

EASY ON AND OFF CLOTHING — *Simple, comfortable* clothing with snaps on the front or bottom are the *only* way to go while your multiples are infants. With twins as an example, between dressing and diaper changes, you will be wrestling with clothing about 20 times a day. Add wiggly babies to the picture, and you will be looking for the nearest garbage can to house those once adorable "foo-foo" outfits!

• • •

6 ONESIES PER CHILD — You will be changing these in "twosies" or "threesies." Onesies (also called "bodysuits") are one-piece t-shirts with snaps at the crotch. They provide an extra layer of warmth in the winter and they make for perfect "simple" outfits during the summer. (Retail price: about $12/3-pack)

• • •

4 UNDERSHIRTS PER CHILD — Use these until your newborns' umbilical cords fall off. (Retail price: $7–10/3-pack)

• • •

5 PAIRS OF SOCKS PER CHILD — Your best bet is to buy same-style white socks (with elasticity) for your children. Don't get caught up with matching socks with outfits. If you do, you will have a drawer full of socks you rarely use. If you choose something other than same-style white socks, don't forget the time it will take to find the mate when you do the laundry. (Retail price: $2–4/pair) *NOTE: Avoid "booties." I think I finally figured out why they are called "booties" — if you purchase them, it won't be long until you boot them out of your house. Most won't stay on tiny feet unless you duct tape them.*

• • •

4–5 SLEEPER OUTFITS PER CHILD — These are those snuggly long sleeve, long pant, one-piece outfits that you always see babies wearing. Most can be used as day or nightwear, but are most often used at night. (Retail price: varies)

• • •

2–3 INFANT CAPS PER CHILD — Great for helping to maintain newborn's body temperature, even in the summer months. Particularly useful for preemies. Ask the hospital staff for extras before you leave. (Retail price: $3–5 each)

• • •

5–6 RECEIVING BLANKETS PER CHILD — Avoid buying these in advance of your shower, because they are a very popular gift item. Before you leave the hospital, ask your nurse to show you how to properly swaddle your infants in them. (Retail price: about $10/pack) *NOTE: Look for Kiddopotamus "Swaddle Me" blankets. They come in various sizes, including preemie. Swaddle Me blankets are great because unlike generic receiving blankets, they actually stay folded, and you can change babies' diapers without completely unswaddling them. They are more expensive, but worth every penny for the convenience.*

• • •

BLANKETS — You will need a small warm blanket for each child. Also, look for one of the cheapest queen-sized ones you can find. Use this blanket as a carpet protector (from drools and spit-ups), as well as when you spend time outdoors. If you already own an old large comforter or blanket, hold on it to and scratch this off your registry. *NOTE: If you plan to spend lots of time outdoors, it may be worth buying a water-resistant, Tuffo blanket* (www.tuffo.com). *(Retail price: $39.95) For larger families, shop at* www.mambeblankets.com *and choose your size. (Retail price: $25–250)*

• • •

1 JACKET OR BUNTING PER CHILD (?) — For use in colder months/ climates. *NOTE: Avoid snowsuits (see NOT-SO-HANDY THINGS for more information).*

• • •

Toiletries:

BABY TOILETRIES — Don't go crazy registering for baby toiletries. Although you are expecting multiples, don't think that you will need a closet full of this stuff. Things such as large bottles of shampoos and lotions may last months, not weeks. Some toiletries and quantities (for twins *or* triplets) to have might be:

- 1 large bottle baby shampoo
- 2 bottles liquid bath soap (avoid bars of soap)
- 3 bottles infant pain reliever (Tylenol)
- 1 bottle infant gas drops (Mylicon)
- 1 container diaper rash ointment
- 1 tube antibiotic cream

- 1 bottle electrolyte solution (Pedialite) — prevents dehydra-
  tion when vomiting/diarrhea
- 1 bottle rubbing alcohol (for umbilical cord care)
- 1 large bag cotton balls
- 1 large container of Q-tips
- 2 large containers of dye free/fragrance free liquid laundry
  soap

Other than the few items listed, you won't need too many toiletries to get you started. *NOTE: Many new mothers never use baby powder, baby lotion and baby oil, although they are marketed as baby "essentials." If you think you might use them, add them to your list, but buy no more than one of each.*

• • •

1 BABY GROOMING KIT — These usually include a hairbrush, comb, nail clippers and a nail file. (Retail price: $9–35)

• • •

1 NASAL BULB — Used for suctioning gunk out of little noses. (Retail price: $2–3)

• • •

1 THERMOMETER — There are three basic kinds: Ear, rectal, and now a forehead thermometer. I highly recommend the Exergen Temporal Forehead Thermometer because you won't have to fuss with clenched little butt cheeks! It's the quickest, most gentle thermometer available and it measures temperature with a quick scan across the forehead. It's more accurate than an ear thermometer, and at least as accurate as a rectal. (Retail price: $30–50)

• • •

1 INFANT BATHTUB AND FOAM BATH CUSHION — This is not an absolute necessity, but very convenient. (Retail price: $15–30)

• • •

6 ADULT-SIZED WASHCLOTHS PER CHILD — Register for soft, regular washcloths, not baby washcloths. They are larger and perfect for baths, clean ups, and can also be used as burp cloths. If you get baby washcloths as a gift, thank the gift-giver, and then return them! You will need to do twice the washing and wiping with these itsy-bitsy, impractical things. (Retail price: about $10/pack)

• • •

2 HOODED BATH TOWELS PER CHILD — Nice to have, however, any bath towel will suffice. (Retail price: varies)

• • •

Travel:

1 MINIVAN OR SPORT UTILITY VEHICLE — Put one on your registry, cross your fingers, and see what happens (just don't get your hopes up)!

• • •

1 DOUBLE STROLLER (?) — See section on THINGS THAT STROLL for more information. (Retail price: varies)

• • •

1 TRIPLE STROLLER (?) — See section on THINGS THAT STROLL for more information. (Retail price: varies)

• • •

1 INFANT CAR SEAT PER CHILD — Figure out what stroller you want before you buy a car seat! See section on CAR SEAT SAFETY AND TIPS for more information. (Retail price: $50–200)

• • •

1–2 INFANT HEAD SUPPORT(S)/CAR SEAT INSERTS PER CHILD — When your babies first come home from the hospital, and for the first few months, they will need support for their wobbly heads as they sit in their car seats. Head supports are a worthwhile purchase because they can also be used for added security in strollers and baby swings. Consider two per child if you plan to use them for these purposes. (Retail price: $10–15)

• • •

1 BABY CARRIER (?) — Tot Tenders has "Maximom" baby carriers specially designed for twins and triplets (birth–30 pounds). If you have twins, see if you can borrow (or buy) one from another mother of multiples, because they are expensive and your babies will outgrow them in no time. If you prefer to buy new, you can find these online in just about every shop that sells products for multiples. (Retail price about $98) There is also a new "Weego Twin" carrier *(www.weego.com)* on the market that may be of interest. (Retail price: $129) *NOTE: Although there is a Maximom carrier designed for triplets, I would not recommend using one. They can be cumbersome, and if you wear one, prepare to be mistaken for part of a circus act! You will be quite a spectacle with three*

babies strapped to your chest and back, along with 14 arms and legs that will be thrashing about (including our own). This product is much better suited for those with twins. Yet another thought: Use a single carrier instead of a double or triple. Since there is usually (at least) one fussy baby in the house, you can use the single carrier to sooth the baby who needs to be held while you attend to other domestic duties. Although the single carrier is only useful for one baby, you might be surprised at how convenient it is!

· · ·

1 DIAPER BAG — Think about your personality before registering for a diaper bag. If you like to travel light, consider a smaller bag. If you are the type to carry everything "just in case," buy a large bag. Once you have considered size, determine if you are the type that tosses things into your purse, or meticulously puts everything in its place. If you toss, think about a bag with few compartments, and if you are meticulous, a bag with lots of compartments. There are a wide variety of styles and price ranges, so consider all of this while shopping. Shopping online for a diaper bag might be a good idea. Baby superstores have a limited variety, especially if you are looking for a stylish, high-end bag. *NOTE: If you like large bags, look for a "Duo Double" diaper bag by Skip Hop. They are specially designed to fit side-by-side strollers. Even if you don't have a side-by-side stroller, they are great for parents with multiples. (Available at www.justmultiples.com for $79.95).*

· · ·

Entertainment/Gear:

1 ACTIVITY PAD/GYMINI — These multi-colored floor pads offer hours of entertainment for the first few months. Your babies will be able to use the same one because they should both/all fit underneath as they play with the dangling toys that hang above them. (Retail price: $35–60). *NOTE: Tiny Love makes a cute "Noah's Ark Gymini Deluxe." You can find this online at www.amazon.com under "toys and games."*

· · ·

1 BABY SWING — Start out with one and see if your babies like it. Some babies love swings while others don't. (Retail price: $50–110)

• • •

1 VIBRATING BOUNCY SEAT PER CHILD — One for each child isn't essential, but it might help to know that most parents who use them, swear by them. Many claim that they would "never eat dinner" if each child did not have a bouncy seat. (Retail price: about $30)

• • •

1 BASSINET PER CHILD (?) — Convenient if you can borrow them (Retail price: $30–200), because your babies will out grow them in 3–4 months. If you really want bassinets, buy Pack 'n Play's with bassinets built into them. *NOTE: Graco now has a "Pack 'n Play with Twin Bassinets." This Pack 'n Play features double bassinets and it also has an extra large play area for napping or playing as babies grow. (Retail price: $199) You can find this product at Babies "R" Us or visit* www.gracobaby.com *to find a retailer.*

• • •

1 PACK 'N PLAY PER CHILD (?) — These are smaller-scale rectangular playpens intended for containing one child (primarily used for sleeping away from home). If you are the traveling type who enjoys weekend trips or visiting relatives, a Pack 'n Play for each child is recommended. If you live in a two-story home, these will also come in handy for napping on the first floor (at some point you will get tired of carrying your growing babies up and down steps for naps). (Retail price: about $60)

• • •

1 PLAYPEN (?) — Probably not, unless you want a great place to toss your children's toys. Chances are good you will have childproofed an entire room in your home and gated it. If gating is not an option, look for a Superyard (and XT Extension Kit) instead. (Retail price: $60–90) *NOTE: See section on HANDY THINGS for more information about the Superyard.*

• • •

Feeding (bottle):
FORMULA (?) — You will need formula if you plan to bottle feed or supplement your breast milk, but don't buy it in advance! Many newborns need to try different formulas before they find one that suits them. Your pediatrician will suggest which formula to use. See FORMULA AND OTHER FLUIDS for more information.

• • •

1 TWO-QUART POURING PITCHER WITH LID — For parents who plan to use liquid-concentrate or powdered formula. (Retail price: $5–20)

• • •

8 – (8 OZ) BOTTLES PER CHILD — See NOT-SO-BASIC BOTTLE FEEDING BASICS for more information. (Retail price: $1–5)

• • •

4 – (4 OZ) BOTTLES PER CHILD — These aren't essential, but a few are nice to travel with. (Retail price: $1–3)

• • •

1 BOTTLE BRUSH — Useful for cleaning the bottoms of bottles, particularly those you discover under couches, when it's anyone's guess as to how long they've been fermenting. (Retail price: about $5)

• • •

1–2 BOTTLE DRYING RACK(S) — A good place to store and dry bottles after cleaning. Buy one rack for twins; and consider two for triplets. (Retail price: about $10)

• • •

1–2 PLASTIC DISHWASHER BASKET(S) — These hold small objects such as bottle tops, nipples and pacifiers. You will need at least one for twins, and possibly two for triplets. (Retail price: $5–10) *NOTE: Look for Prince Lionheart's "toddler" dishwasher basket —— it's the largest basket around, and you need not have toddlers to use it.*

• • •

5 MEDIUM SIZED BIBS PER CHILD — Look for bibs that have vinyl backing and snaps, and avoid Velcro and ties. A determined child can easily pull apart Velcro, and you won't want to spend time tying ties, or have to cut them when you can't get the knot out. (Retail price: about $6) *NOTE: Avoid bibs that are complete upper body covers. When it comes to bibs and shielding multiples, the simpler the better.*

• • •

Feeding (breast):
1 EZ-2-NURSE TWINS BREASTFEEDING PILLOW — Available in foam ($48) or inflatable ($40) online at *www.doubleblessings.com*. See section on A BRIEFING ABOUT BREASTFEEDING for detailed instructions on how to use this product.

• • •

1 DOUBLE BREAST PUMP (?) — Consider renting (not buying) a "hospital grade" double breast pump (Medela and Ameda are the most popular). *NOTE: If your babies are born near full term, and you plan to breastfeed exclusively, a pump may not be necessary. Speak to your lactation consultant before you rent a breast pump. She will be able to help you determine if you need one, and if so, which one to use, and where to find it. ANOTHER NOTE: You can also find out where to rent these products by going to the manufacturers' websites, www.medela.com and www.ameda.com.*

• • •

2–4 NURSING BRAS (?) — For support, dryness protection during post-feeding, and easy access. (Retail price: $10–38) *NOTE: Wait until your milk comes in to buy these because your breast size will change.*

• • •

2–4 NURSING T-SHIRTS — Great for daytime and for sleeping at night. (Retail price: $20–35) *NOTE: Shop for nursing shirts with overlapping slits for easier access.*

• • •

1 NURSING COVER/SHAWL (?) — Convenient, but not essential, unless you prefer a bit more privacy. (Retail price: $25–35)

• • •

2–4 LOOSE NIGHT GOWNS — Find a few loose, comfortable ones. (Retail price: varies) *NOTE: Pass up on "nursing nightgowns" if you plan to feed two babies at the same time. The slits in them can shift to one side or the other when attempting to feed two. Regular button-down pajamas are probably best for this purpose.*

• • •

6 BOXES — DISPOSABLE BREAST PADS — For leaky boobs. (Retail price: $8–10) *NOTE: Be careful not to overstock on breast pads because some mothers find their breasts do not leak. Also, steer clear of washable pads. The last thing you will want to do is more laundry!*

• • •

1 JAR NIPPLE CREAM — For sore, cracked nipples. (Retail price: varies)

• • •

2 CASES BOTTLED WATER — Keep a couple cases of bottled water in your pantry. You will get very thirsty nursing!

. . .

VITAMINS — Speak to your doctor or lactation consultant about what to take, as well as recommended dosage. Most women continue to take their prenatal vitamins, as well as additional calcium (if they are not getting enough in their diet).

. . .

HEALTHY SNACKS — Have some on hand that are easily accessible throughout the day.

. . .

OTHER BREASFEEDING SUPPLIES — There will be other products to purchase if you plan to pump or supplement your breast milk (which will be the case if your babies spend any time in the NICU). These include bottles, nipples, storage bags and/or storage bottles. Speak to your lactation consultant about whether she feels these will be necessary, and if so, how many to purchase (this will depend upon your intentions).

. . .

Miscellaneous:
1 BABY MEMORY BOOK PER CHILD — These will be cherished for years to come. A book for each child will remind your children of their individuality, and will also be convenient when they become adults and want to take their book with them. (Retail price: about $15–20 per book) *NOTE: For memory books devoted to twins, look for my new book, "Twice Upon a Time" (www.justmultiples.com) or "Twins" (www.twinsmagazine.com). Both are sold as a set (one for each child). If you have triplets, your best bet might be to put together a scrapbook or buy any baby book for each of your babies. There aren't any memory books written for triplets that I am aware of.*

. . .

1 DAILY SCHEDULE BOOK — Since you will soon be juggling more than one newborn, it will be important to keep track of feedings, diapering, medications, naps, and other information. A schedule book will be helpful for caregivers and for discussing progress with the pediatrician. You can create your own schedule book (see sample in the SIMPLE THINGS THAT SIMPLIFY section) or, if you have better things to do with your time, look for *Double Time* and *Triple Time* schedule books online at *www.justmultiples.com*. (Retail price: $12.95/3-month supply)

•••

2 PACIFIERS PER CHILD — Why not? They are small and inexpensive. This is not something you should "buy later." Have a couple on hand, even if you *swear* you won't use them! Some babies have strong sucking urges, while others don't. If you end up not using them, you can always return them. (Retail price: about $2)

•••

2 DIAPER PAILS — You will need more than one, especially if you live in a two-story house. The Safety 1st Easy Saver (or Odorless Diaper Pail) are simple and decent-sized. (Retail price: $15) Another option, and probably the best option is the Diaper Champ by Baby Trend. (Retail price: about $30) All of these products use regular kitchen bags. *NOTE: You might also want to splurge on a new garbage can and designate it for "diapers only." If you think you fill your garbage can quickly now, just wait! Your family will soon become a major contributor to your local landfill.*

•••

3 BOXES — TALL "KITCHEN" TRASH BAGS — Start out with three large boxes if you plan to buy diaper pails that use them, and shop at whole-sale stores to find larger quantities and better prices.

•••

TRUCKLOADS OF DIAPERS — Have a general idea of what brand of diaper you might use, and stock up on about three weeks worth to get you started (sizes: newborn and size 1). Keep about 280 "newborn" diapers on hand for twins and about 420 for triplets. Have a week's worth of "size 1" as well (twins: 140/triplets: 210). (Retail price: about $20/large pack or $35/case) *NOTE: The amount of diapers I have indicated is a generous approximation and assumes that you will use ten diapers a day per child. Most newborns go through about 8–10 diapers per day.*

•••

PREEMIE DIAPERS (?) — If you think you might need preemie diapers, my suggestion is to wait. If you have preemie babies, the hospital will be providing care and diapers for a while. If you feel more comfortable having a supply, buy no more than a week's worth (twins: 140/triplets: 210). *NOTE: The best place to find preemie diapers is Babies "R" Us because most other stores don't stock them.*

• • •

1 CASE — BABY WIPES — You will need truckloads of these as well. You will use them for tiny heinies, adorable faces, sticky hands, and lots of other messes. (Retail price: $2–$5/container)

• • •

8–10 BURP CLOTHS PER CHILD — "Real" burp cloths are cute, but can also be very expensive when you need to buy lots of them. Cloth diapers are better for this purpose, and can be found in just about any store that sells baby products. (Retail price: $10–12/12 pack)

Please see APPENDIX 1 in the back of this book for a summary of products discussed on the previous pages. For convenience, cut out the pages, or take this book with you when you register for your baby shower. Remember to modify the list to suit your needs.

NURSERY
NECESSITIES AND NON-NECESSITIES

The Internet is flooded with delightful nursery sets and décor. Shop online if you would like an alternative to what the baby superstores offer. If you are on a budget, think twice before spending too much on your babies' nursery. If the theme is too "babyish," you will find yourself redecorating in no time. Look for a theme that will last a few years. If you do, the small fortune you spend won't be so difficult to swallow, or might even be justified! *NOTE: Parents of multiples don't get as much use out of their nurseries as parents of singletons, who often rotate their babies in and out of them on an individual basis.*

• • •

Furniture:
NOTE: If an item on the following list does not have "PER CHILD" next to it, the number indicated is the amount recommended for both/all of your babies. If an item has a question mark (?) following it, it may not be necessary.

1 CRIB PER CHILD — Although your babies may share one at first, ultimately there will be no avoiding a crib for each child. If space is an issue, look at *www.babytrilogy.com* for a uniquely designed corner crib option, or *www.cribs.com* for "Little Miss Liberty" round cribs that connect and save space in smaller nurseries. Or, if you are in desperate need of nursery space, look to *www.daycareuniverse.com* for a stackable crib option. Daycare Universe sells Windsor Stackable Cribs that stack in sets of two. If you have triplets, you might think about a stackable crib for two and a single crib. *NOTE: The Windsor cribs are smaller than regular cribs (you will need to move your children into beds much sooner if you purchase them).*

• • •

1 DRESSER — Save money and space by purchasing only one (with at least one large drawer per child). Everything should fit (as long as you also have closet space for additional clothing). Even if you plan to have two (or three) nurseries, you will only need one dresser. In fact, one dresser and one closet will be easier to go to for all the clothing, versus running into different nurseries whenever you need to dress your babies.

• • •

1 CHANGING TABLE/STATION (?) — Certainly nice to have for storing diapers, wipes, and lotions, but believe it or not, having one is not essential! With multiples, you will probably find a floor, crib, or bed to be more convenient for diapering. Another option is to buy a changing pad and place it on top of a dresser. Keep the lotions on top and the diapers in an extra drawer or nearby shelf.

• • •

1–2 (PADDED) GLIDER(S) (?) — If you plan to bottle feed, you will probably be spending most of your days (and nights) in these chairs, so make sure it's comfortable! If you can spring for another, consider two. Keep one in the babies' nursery and a second one in a room where you spend most of your time (no silly, not the kitchen!). (Retail price: $100–800) *NOTE: If you breastfeed, you will probably find that the nursing pillow you use does not fit between the arms of this chair. As a result, you won't use your glider much, other than to relax in and rock your babies. Consider whether the price tag is worth it in this case.*

• • •

1 OTTOMAN (?) — Most are sold separately as a glider accessory. If space and money are an issue, do without one and save $80–200. I never used an ottoman and was very comfortable (I opted for two gliders). *NOTE: Along with gliders, breastfeeding mothers often find ottomans uncomfortable (or unnecessary) for nursing.*

• • •

1 SMALL TABLE LAMP W/ SHADE (?) — Good for reading bedtime stories and setting a bedtime routine. If you want one, purchase one with a dimmer. (Retail price: $15–40) *NOTE: Lampshades are sometimes offered as a matching accessory to crib bedding.*

• • •

Crib Bedding:

CRIB COMFORTERS/QUILTS (?) — Crib comforters and quilts are appealing and aggressively marketed, but the fact is, they don't belong in infant cribs. If you purchase them, hang them on the wall as nursery décor until it's safe to put blankets in the crib. (Retail price: varies)

• • •

CRIB BUMPERS (?) — These are a nice accent to a crib and might prevent your child from getting a bruise or bump, but they are also an added expense and are thought to be a potential safety hazard. It's important to remember that as soon as your babies are able to stand in their cribs, you should remove the bumpers because they make it easier for children to climb out. (Retail price: varies)

• • •

1 CRIB SKIRT PER CHILD (?) — Often sold with crib sets. Crib skirts add a nice finishing touch to a crib, and if you use them, you can throw storage under the crib(s), and no one will see the clutter! (Retail price: varies)

• • •

2–3 FITTED CRIB SHEETS PER CHILD — Buy pre-washed cotton sheets. If they aren't, you will be buying more in no time! Don't skimp on price for crib sheets. They are safer, a better fit, and you get what you pay for. (Retail price: varies)

• • •

1 FIRM CRIB MATTRESS PER CHILD — These are usually sold separately. Since you will be changing lots of sheets, look first for foam mattresses. They are lighter in weight, and generally less money. (Retail price: $40–120)

...

1 PLASTIC MATTRESS-COVER PER CHILD — You will need these to protect mattresses from leaks, drools and spit-ups. (Retail price: about $20)

...

1–2 SHEET SAVERS PER CHILD — These are what I call "life savers!" Place them under your babies while they sleep, and they stop the fluids from flowing onto the crib sheets. *NOTE: I found Crown Craft's Nojo sheet savers to be one of my most useful shower gifts. They were the perfect size, stayed put, and they saved me from changing and washing sheets all the time. If you can't find Nojo sheet savers, there are other brands that will work just as well. Just make sure they are "crib" sheet savers and not sheet savers intended for regular beds.* (Retail price: $8–10)

...

Other Nursery Stuff:

1 CRIB DIVIDER (?) — If your babies are going to share a crib to start, you might end up in need of a crib divider so that they don't disturb each other as they grow and become more mobile. Since this is not always the case, don't buy one in advance! Wait to see what happens. Many twins and triplets enjoy each other's company and find comfort with their sidekicks. *NOTE: You can find crib dividers online at www. doubleblessings.com.* (Retail price: $30)

...

1 SLEEP POSITIONER PER CHILD — This product cradles newborn babies and keeps them in position on their back while they sleep. Sleep positioners are helpful in reducing the risk of SIDS (Sudden Infant Death Syndrome). (Retail price: $10–30)

...

1 CRIB MOBILE (?) — There will be no need for more than one crib mobile if your babies start out in the same crib. By the time you separate them into their own cribs, you will need to remove the mobile anyway, because they become a safety concern once infants reach five months of age. Besides, at an average price of $30, do you really want two or three of them?

...

1 MUSICAL SLEEP ITEM (?) — Again, you should only need one. (Retail price: about $30) Another option is to record your own voice. If you aren't in desperate need of voice lessons, this is a great alternative!

• • •

1 PLASTIC CRIB MIRROR PER CHILD (?) — Not by any means a neces-sity, but they often give parents some extra time to shower or sleep in the morning. Crib mirrors provide daily entertainment and self-aware-ness as babies stare in quiet amusement at themselves. (Retail price: $15–20)

• • •

1 BABY MONITOR — Some parents exchange their monitors due to interference with other monitors in the neighborhood. Remember to keep the box and receipt until you have used it and are satisfied, and remember to say nice things about your neighbor: If you can hear them, they can hear you! (Retail price: $20–50)

• • •

1 NIGHT LIGHT — Offers the perfect amount for light for "sneaking a peak," changing a diaper, and feeding in the middle of the night. (Retail price: $10) *NOTE: If you find your babies like complete darkness, put the night light in the hallway (for your own use) and buy a small pen light to check on them.*

• • •

1 HUMIDIFIER (?) — Often used in nurseries. Don't buy in advance; wait to see if you need one. (Retail price: $30–60)

• • •

1 CLOTHES HAMPER — For housing all the dirty laundry. If you don't plan to wash clothes every day, buy the largest one you can find. (Retail price: $20–60)

• • •

"ROOM DARKENING" SHADES (?) — These are useful for creating a nighttime atmosphere. They are pricey, but worth a few minutes of extra sleep each morning, afternoon, and night. Room darkening shades are the "Cadillac" of window shades. Don't mistake them for regular window shades. They are thicker and don't let any light into the room (except, of course, when you roll them up!). These can be found in stores that sell window coverings.

• • •

Gear for Grandparents (?):
If grandparents are nearby and plan to care for the babies in their homes, the following is a list of products for them to consider having on hand.

Whether to buy these products or not is optional, and will depend on the amount of time the babies will be spending in their grandparent's homes.

1 jumbo pack — age-appropriate diapers
2 containers — baby wipes
2 (8 oz) bottles per child
1 bottle — infant Tylenol
1 bottle — baby wash
1 bottle — baby shampoo
1 pacifier per child (if using them)
1 infant "portable" swing (this is smaller than regular baby swings)
1 bouncy seat
1 Pack n Play (for sleeping) — parents can bring another along with them (if needed)
1 warm blanket per child
2–3 comfortable, unisex outfits
A few age appropriate toys/books
Use infant car seats for feedings until children are ready for a booster

NOTE: Grandparents will probably also need car seats and a stroller. Since these are bulky, expensive, and not very practical to own unless used all the time, it's probably best if parents bring these with them when needed. If grandparents care for their grandchildren several times a week, it may be worthwhile for them to own this equipment (and increase quantities on the list, as necessary).

"Assemble cribs inside the nursery! My husband spent half of a weekend assembling cribs in our family room, and the other half of the weekend taking them apart so that they fit through the door of the nursery. I never laughed so hard in my life!"
— Allison G. (Mother of 7-month old GGB triplets)

Please see APPENDIX 1 in the back of this book for a summary of products discussed on the previous pages. For convenience, cut out the pages, or take this book with you when you register for your baby shower. Remember to modify the list to suit your needs.

HANDY THINGS

W al-Mart is a great place to shop for baby products. Although their selection is not as vast as Babies "R" Us, just about everything I comparison shopped for was cheaper at Wal-Mart. Price differences ranged from a few cents per product to over $100 for baby furniture. Although Babies "R" Us has a greater selection of baby products, prepare to spend more money if you shop there.

• • •

Wholesale store memberships are valuable. When you go, be careful to buy only what you need. These stores are reasonable when you stick to the essentials. Leave the plastic palm trees, ceramic statues, pitch tents, and cases of chocolate Ring Dings where you found them! Get your diapers, wipes, and only *one* jumbo box of whatever it is you can't live without, and get out!

...

The "Superyard XT" and the "Superyard XT Extension Kit" by North States are plastic containment gates that are handy for keeping your little nomads in one place in your home, backyard, parks, and beaches. They also work well around outdoor grills and Christmas trees. Many parents use this product in place of a traditional playpen, because it offers more space for kids to play in. *NOTE: Going back to the Wal-Mart versus Babies "R" Us comparison: Last time I checked, these products were available online for a total $89.98 at* www.babiesrus.com *and $66.88 at* www.walmart.com *(shipping was also cheaper at Wal-Mart). If you shop at Wal-Mart, you save $23.10! That's a jumbo pack of diapers with $3 left over for a cup of coffee!*

...

When the time comes, you can barricade a staircase, or gate off an entire room with a Configuration Gate ($129.95) and Extension ($39.95) from One Step Ahead *(www.onestepahead.com).* This gating system allows you to create your own configurations, and is perfect for large openings that need to be gated for child safety.

...

Treat yourself to a "Back Jack" floor chair (the best $38 you will spend online at *www.fourgates.com).* Because it will be impossible to hold both/all of your babies, you will probably end up spending most of your time on the floor playing with them — for hours on end! Back Jack floor chairs provide support for your back, are amazingly comfortable, light-weight and portable. You and your back deserve one!

...

Neighbors can come in handy. Give a house key to a neighbor (or two) you trust for those occasions when you find yourself locked out of the house. When this happens, rest assured it will be with wailing infants who have not napped or eaten all day! Another option: If you don't already have one, consider installing a keyless entry into your home.

...

Cordless phones with a call feature are very handy. Check to locate your cordless phone's "call" button (or check to see if it has one). When this button is pressed, it causes the headpiece to send a loud beeping noise to make it easier to locate. This will save you lots of time searching for your misplaced phone, which is bound to happen countless times a day.

• • •

Consider a phone with a hands-free headset. It will allow you to chit-chat and change diapers at the same time. Without one, your life will be full of five-second phone conversations.

• • •

Place a small dry erase board near your kitchen phone. These boards are much better than paper reminders that often get lost in the shuffle.

• • •

Hang a large calendar in your kitchen to highlight appointments, play dates, and other important reminders. You can also use this calendar to take quick notes of your babies' milestones, and transfer the information into their memory books when you have more time. *NOTE: Don't wait until their freshman year of college. By then you will have forgotten a few details!*

• • •

Keep at least two small ice packs in your freezer. You will need them to keep bottles and snacks cool, and will also find that they come in handy for bumps and bruises.

• • •

Plastic powdered formula dispensers are perfect for parents on the go. These containers are convenient for bottle feeders who use powdered formula. They have sections for dispensing enough formula for four pre-measured bottle feedings. They are great for outings, and eliminate the need to keep bottles cold. Those with triplets may want to purchase two. (Retail price: $5)

• • •

Recycle baby wipe boxes. Use them to store crayons and other small items. Start collecting them while your babies are infants. You can use them for storing all sorts of things.

• • •

Desitin and Balmex seem to work best for diaper rash. If you buy Desitin, shop for "Desitin Creamy" (creamy is not as messy). For more serious rashes, parents like Diaper Goop *(www.innopharm.com)* and Boudreaux's Butt Paste *(www.buttpaste.com).*

• • •

Food processors can easily turn people food into baby food. If you don't have one, look for a mini-processor. Use extra ice cube trays to freeze your leftovers, or buy a few small plastic containers for storage.

• • •

Jar openers are a useful time-saving tool. Although baby food jars are tiny and cute, some can be an absolute bear to open!

• • •

Have you spent quality time with your broom lately? If not, take a good look at it. If it's not a sturdy broom in good condition, invest in one that is. You can expect to sweep your kitchen floor at least 1,460 times a year (well, at least you should!) while your children are young. You will need a quality broom and dustpan if you plan to spend less time in the kitchen and more time with your kids. *NOTE: If you would like to spend even less time in your kitchen, purchase a Shark Cordless Sweeper. (Retail price: about $70) The Shark is super lightweight, a snap to use, and picks up everything from pet hair to cheerios. You can find it at Target, and many other stores.*

• • •

Dust busters are handy for picking up crumbs from tables, floors and carpeting. They are perfect for small messes.

• • •

Zud is an amazing all-purpose cleaner. It cleans just about everything other cleaners can't. Zud may be difficult to find because not all grocery stores carry it, but it's worth the search. It comes in a bright yellow and blue bottle.

• • •

Do you believe in magic? You will, once you use Mr. Clean Magic Erasers! If you have scuffs, crayon, or other marks on your walls or baseboards, this Mr. Clean product magically erases them. Magic Erasers come in a box and are sold in most grocery stores.

• • •

Look around your house to see if you have a few small plastic buckets (inexpensive waste paper baskets are best). When one gets a virus, everyone usually gets the virus! At least two buckets are good to have on hand.

• • •

Baby medicine dispensers are helpful for all of those times you will need to give undiluted medicine to your babies. *NOTE: A few brands to shop for are the Baby Nipple Medicator by Munchkin, the Medibottle by Sav-iBaby, or the Medicine Dispenser Pacifier by One Step Ahead.*

...

Most mothers agree that ibuprofen products, such as Infant and Children's Motrin, work best for reducing fevers. These products work faster, last longer, and bring fevers down farther than other over-the-counter pain medications. *NOTE: If your babies are younger than six months, acetaminophen (such as Infant Tylenol) is the safest medication for this purpose. Infants should not be given ibuprofen until they are at least six months old, or without a doctor's approval.*

...

Nighttime vapor plugs are a must for winter congestion and sniffles. Just plug one in and your kids should sleep more soundly. *NOTE: Look for Sudacare or Pediacare products. (Retail price: $20–25)*

...

In colder months, infant snuggle sacks are a great alternative to snowsuits and other outerwear when babies need to take a quick trip in the car. Snuggle sacks keep babies warm in their car seat carriers. *NOTE: Kiddopotamus has two styles: the Cozy-Up Carrier Cover ($20), and the Faux Shearling Collection ($25). One Step Ahead also offers an Infant Snuggle Sack ($40).*

...

Make bath time safer and more comfortable with a Tub Guard by Joy Products. It slides over the side of your tub, cushions the edges, helps protect babies, and gives parents a comfortable surface to lean on. They also offer a Kneeling Pad. You can find these products in just about any child safety store.

...

Battery testers are very handy. Because so many baby products require batteries, consider buying one. They can be found at Radio Shack *(www.radioshack.com).* Also, look for rechargeable batteries and a battery charger (also found at Radio Shack). Rechargeable batteries are useful for vibrating bouncy seats and battery-operated swings, which will be bouncing and swinging around the clock. If you don't plan to recharge batteries, load up on size "D" batteries whenever you find them on sale.

...

Although they require batteries, most parents choose to use vibrating bouncy seats over standard (manual) bouncy seats. The battery vibration seems to be more helpful in soothing fussy babies.

...

A video camera is essential for creating memories. Put it to good use! If you don't take lots of video when your children are young, you (and your children) will someday regret it.

...

Any of the Fisher-Price Jumperoos are wonderful products to have, because they keep the entire family entertained! Babies love to jump in them, and parents delight in watching. *NOTE: One Jumperoo will be plenty. (Retail price: $60–70)*

...

Find an infant memorabilia box for each child (a simple plastic storage box will do) and put your children's names on them. Place things with sentimental value in them, including first outfits and shoes. One day you will pull out the box and be surprised at how small everything is, and wish your children were that size again.

> "I bought a brag book to keep all the sonogram pictures I accumulated during my pregnancy. This was better than putting them on the refrigerator. I did this with my first child, and many of them got lost."
> — Mary B. (Mother of three, including GG twins)

> "I had an electric tea kettle that I used everyday to sterilize different bottle parts. At the same time, I was known for making myself a cup of tea or hot chocolate to calm the ol' nerves!" — Lindsay S. (Mother of GG twins)

NOT-SO-HANDY THINGS

People who suggest, "I had my children one year apart, so I have a license to tell you what to do." Listen to them, but don't feel the need to heed their advice. Moms of singletons can offer lots of advice, but only a mother of multiples truly understands your challenges and can offer practical advice that really helps.

• • •

The "know it all" who exists in every family. Not your family? Yes, your family! Don't let this person bother you. It may help to know that just about every family has one!

• • •

A budget. Plan to spend much more than you ever imagined. It's wise to keep a budget in mind and try to stick to it, but chances are you will blow it with multiples!

• • •

Pre-washed baby clothing. Most new mothers pre-wash clothing prior to putting the outfits on their infants. Pre-washing is a good idea, but it may not be wise to launder everything. Although many of the outfits will match and be adorable (except for that *one* from Aunt "What's-her-name"), you will probably end up using very few "adorable" outfits in the first several weeks because you will be swaddling your babies. Look through your stash and find a handful of your favorites and pre-wash them. Keep the tags on all the others and wash them as needed.

• • •

Diaper Genies are a fantastic product — if you have a singleton! There are other more practical options for housing your heaps of diapers (see section on THINGS TO CONSIDER/THINGS TO AVOID for more information).

• • •

Cloth diapers. During a recent conversation with my mother, she said she used cloth diapers in the 1960s because she had no choice. As she described her experience in detail, I couldn't help but think, what a hassle, and what a filthy mess it must have been with twins! We have come a long way since the 60s. Do you really want to use the same diapering technique my mother used? Your choice, but I vote to put them on the "not handy" list. If you want to use cloth diapers, use them as burp cloths instead. *NOTE: If you still have an interest in using cloth diapers, look up "diaper services" in your local phone book, or visit www.earthybirthymama.com.*

• • •

Germs. Make a valiant effort to get rid of as many as you can before (and after) your babies come home. Doing this will help to keep your entire family healthy. Did you know that (according to a study conducted by the University of Arizona) phones can have up to 400 times more germs than a toilet seat? It's true! This is the case because most toilets are scrubbed every now and then, and the majority of phones aren't. Use disinfecting wipes (or paper towels and rubbing alcohol), to wipe down your phones, and disinfect all high-trafficked areas, such as banisters, doorknobs, light switches, changing tables, and of course, bathrooms. Also, hand washing should become a regular habit. To ensure hands become germ-free, squirt a generous amount of soap onto your paws and rub-a-dub-dub for a good 15 seconds before rinsing, especially before picking up your newborn babies!

...

Co-sleepers (a bedside bassinette). Good luck attaching more than one to your bed, and if you succeed, good luck sleeping! If you really feel the need to sleep next to your newborns, place a twin mattress in their nursery, and sleep in *their* room. If you do this, at least one parent will get some sleep!

...

Manual wind-up swings. Having one is acceptable, but more than one does nothing but wind up parents!

...

Walkers. Not only are they potentially dangerous, multiples often run over the bare feet of other siblings who are not in them. Their name is also a misnomer. There are studies that suggest walkers might actually delay walking. These products are probably not worth any added convenience. *NOTE: According to the National Safe Kids Campaign, there are more than 6,000 walker-related injuries reported annually in the United States.*

...

Laundry detergents specifically marketed for infants are not necessarily the best option due to their price. Save money by choosing any fragrance-free, dye-free brand.

...

Wipe warmers. Do you heat your toilet paper? If you were lucky enough to have gotten one as a shower gift, return it for something more useful, or better yet, offer it to a mother of a singleton! Joking aside, not only are they not worth the money, many have been recalled for safety reasons.

...

Stuffed animals. If you think you will soon be outnumbered with twins or triplets, just wait until the stuffed animals that go along with them start rolling in. Just about every gift you receive will either be a stuffed animal, or have one attached to the box. If you are expecting twins, pre-pare to do as Noah once did: Welcome every animal by two into your home. Avoid buying these adorable things. Stuffed animals that were once "too cute" can turn ugly!

•••

Infant snowsuits. Unless you live in Antarctica, multiple infant snowsuits are not practical for a number a number of reasons:

- They are difficult to get on and take off.
- They make it difficult to strap your babies into their car seats.
- Babies often overheat wearing them.
- You will rarely use them.
- There are better options.

Consider fleece buntings if you plan to spend time outdoors in the winter months.

•••

Books with paper pages. These books don't have a very long shelf life with very young children. Consider buying "chunky" books until your children are old enough to know not to pull pages out of their bedtime stories.

"I made the mistake of refusing second-hand clothing and baby equipment when I was expecting. As a first-time mother, I wanted 'new' products. Soon after giving birth, I realized how quickly my twins outgrow things — not to mention how expensive they are!"
— Kathryn K. (Mother of 2-year-old BB twins)

THINGS THAT STROLL

Now that you have a better idea of what you will need, you're probably wondering, "Two of this, six of that, dozens of these...for goodness sake, isn't there *anything* I need just one of?" Well, yes, there is something you will need one of (maybe two, depending on your needs) – an enormous stroller built for two (or three). It looks nothing like that cutesy single-seater your neighbor has and it's quite the piece of equipment. This will be one of your most important purchases, so be sure to do your research, and don't make a hasty decision! Shopping for a stroller should be similar to the way you would go about shopping for a car (with less haggling). The "set of wheels" you purchase should be one you will be happy with, and will be able to use for about four years.

• • •

Although there aren't as many stroller choices for multiples, it seems the more seats a stroller has, the more confusing and expensive the purchase becomes. No matter what you read or who you talk to, your head will spin, and at the end of the day, you will probably still not have an answer to the million-dollar question, "Which stroller should I buy?" This chapter will not answer this question, but should help you to make a more informed decision.

• • •

There are two basic types of strollers for multiples:

- *front/back* (more commonly known as "inline" or "tandem")
- *side-by-side*

If you ask 100 parents of twins which stroller type they prefer, about half of them will tell you tandem and the other half will tell you side-by-side. A few years ago, if you asked the same 100 parents, most would tell you they preferred tandem strollers, because just about all of the side-by-side choices were too wide for most doorways and were not easy to shop with. Now that many (but not all) side-by-side double strollers have a narrower design, squeezing through doorways and aisles is no longer the problem it used to be. If you ask parents of triplets which stroller type they prefer, you will get a very different response. The vast majority will tell you they prefer tandem because there's no way anyone can fit a side-by-side triple stroller through a standard doorway, unless they fold it up first! *NOTE: If one of your favorite pastimes is shopping, look for a stroller that has a width of 31" or less. Anything wider will slow you down and will not fit through standard doorways.*

• • •

Take a moment to review the following comparisons between tandem (front-back) and side-by-side strollers:

TANDEM (FRONT/BACK) STROLLERS	
ADVANTAGES	DISADVANTAGES
Fits through all doorways	Some can be difficult to steer/turn
Better fit through narrow spaces	Many have restricted view and leg room in the back seat(s)
Not as obvious you are pushing multiples	Some seats don't recline very far
Children seem to "stay put" and don't ask to get out as often	Restricted space in the back if front seat is reclined
Some have forward or rear facing seat options	Children sometimes argue over who sits in the front/back
Many offer "stadium seating" for a better view	Generally not as much storage capacity in the bins
	Storage bins are often not as accessible
	On some models, seats need to be removed to put in car
	Triples tend to flip if your don't balance the weight when placing your children in them

SIDE-BY-SIDE STROLLERS	
ADVANTAGES	DISADVANTAGES
Children have a better view	Attracts more attention
Usually more storage capacity in the bins	More of a challenge to get through doors and small spaces
Easier to access storage bins	Children sometimes hang forward when they are upset
Babies generally not as bored with a sibling sitting next to them	Some models are too narrow for older toddlers
Usually lighter in weight	Some doubles do not fit through doorways
Easier to fold	Triples do not fit through doorways
Generally better for active people	

• • •

Try to keep an open mind about which stroller type you prefer, and before you begin to "shop" anywhere for a stroller, first, gather as much information as you can by visiting all of the manufacturers' websites that are within your budget. This will give you an excellent idea of what is available, regardless of where you end up making your purchase. Indeed this will be time consuming, but it will be worth your while to do your homework…in a systematic, organized way. *NOTE: A list of manufacturers is located in* **APPENDIX 2** *in the back of this book.*

• • •

I recommend that you visit the manufacturers' websites first for the following reasons:

1) You will find more product information, pictures, and sometimes instructional videos.
2) Manufacturers are continually coming out with new products. Their websites are usually the first to display the newest strollers available.
3) You will see the entire line of products the company has to offer, not just a sampling (including color options and accessories).
4) You can call their customer service line and ask lots of questions.
5) Manufacturers' websites usually have listings of their authorized retailers (both online and local brick and mortar stores). *NOTE: If you buy a new stroller over the Internet, make sure you purchase the product from one of the manufacturer's authorized dealers. If you don't, there is a chance you may not be covered under the manufacturer's warranty agreement (beware of eBay)!*
6) If you take the time to visit all of the manufacturer's sites listed in this book, you will have seen just about all of the double and triple strollers on the market.

The only information you won't get from most manufacturers' websites is pricing, because the majority do not sell directly to the consumer. Use the price guide found with the list of manufacturers (**APPENDIX 2** in the back of this book) for more information about stroller pricing.

• • •

When reviewing the list of manufacturers, look first at the sites that offer strollers you are shopping for (double, triple, etc.). Next, browse the other websites to ensure you have not missed something, including the list of companies that offer single strollers, and those that are sold outside of the United States. Manufacturers are continually expanding their markets and coming out with new products, so it's anyone's guess as to when a new stroller for multiples might be available for purchase.

NOTE: As I write this, Bugaboo does not offer a double stroller, although they are planning to come out with one in 2008.

• • •

Once you've gathered information and have narrowed down your choices, next, visit several consumer review websites. Unlike most stores that sell the strollers, consumer review websites will give you unbiased reviews from those who have actually used the strollers you are considering. Another great thing about consumer review sites: Most also offer price comparisons, which will give you a good idea of what you will end up paying for the product. *NOTE: Keep in mind that the businesses that pop up on review websites are not the only ones selling the strollers! They are part of a merchant network and have paid for advertising. Use consumer review sites for feedback and information gathering, not so much for "the place" to shop.*

• • •

Some of the more popular consumer review websites are:

www.baby-gaga.com
www.consumerreview.com
www.epinions.com
www.shopping.com
www.wize.com

• • •

After you've further reduced your options, based upon which strollers have gotten acceptable reviews, confirm this by asking other mothers of multiples on any of the multiples message boards (such as *www. twinsmagazine.com, www.twinstuff.com* or *www.tripletconnection.org*). Limit your questions to avoid getting replies for every stroller ever built. Come up with a handful of five or fewer strollers and ask for feedback on specific makes and models.

• • •

The following checklist should help when comparing two or more strollers you can't make a decision about. Review the list, and consider buying the stroller that ends up with the most "yes" checks. If some of the questions don't apply, do not matter to you, or you are not sure about, leave them blank for an equal comparison. If you have specific questions which are important to you, call the manufacturer and speak to its customer service department. Representatives will be able to answer (just about) all of your questions. Don't rely on the business selling the stroller to give you the best information, especially online retailers. Many online businesses don't even stock their strollers, because they participate in a drop-ship program with the manufacturer.

Stroller Comparison Chart

#1:_____

#2:_____

#3:_____

#4:_____

	STROLLER			
	#1	#2	#3	#4
	Yes? ✔	Yes? ✔	Yes? ✔	Yes? ✔
The stroller is within our budget				
Sturdy, with an adequate weight limit (38+ pounds per seat)				
Easy to fold/unfold (no need to disassemble to fit in car)				
Folded dimensions will fit in my vehicle				
Seats face in the direction I prefer (facing in/facing out/dual facing)				
I can lift it to put in my car, or carry it up stairs (< 40 pounds for petite parents)				
Easy handling (turning/steering)				
Handlebar is high enough (or adjustable) for both parents (36+ inches, for taller parents)				
Adequate storage capacity in the basket				
Storage basket is easily accessible				
Offers sun canopies/ample shade for babies				
Seats recline down to at least 30 degrees (for newborn napping)				
Wheels will accommodate the terrain I will be using it on				
Front wheel(s) swivel(s)/ lock(s) or are fixed in place, as I like				
Stroller style is suitable for the environment I plan to use it in (city, country, beach)				
Stroller fits though most doorways (< 31" width)				
Overall size of the stroller is acceptable (I have room to store it)				
Style is what I prefer (tandem vs. side-by-side)				
Design is what I intend to use it for (jogging, strolling, traveling, shopping, errands, etc.)				
Accessories are available that I might use (cup holder, rain canopy, etc.)				
I believe my babies will be comfortable in this stroller				
Manufacturer offers at least a one-year warranty				

Comes with a double car seat adapter (most models do not)				
Positive customer feedback				
I like the color (and so does my husband!)				
I can see myself pushing this stroller four years from now				
Other				
Other				
TOTAL "YES" Checks:				

• • •

Once you've made a decision about which stroller to buy, go back online and shop for the best price. Review the following websites, and if these aren't enough, "Google" and "Yahoo" the specific make and model as well:

www.best-price.com
www.calibex.com
www.consumerreview.com
www.dealtime.com
www.mysimon.com
www.pricegrabber.com
www.pricescan.com
www.shopping.com

• • •

No matter where you purchase your stroller (whether online or locally), don't forget to compare shipping fees and sales tax. In some cases shipping and/or sales tax may apply, and in others, it won't. So, keep these potential costs in mind when shopping for the best price. Once you find the right price and where to buy the stroller, make your purchase.

• • •

Some other things to consider while stroller shopping:

Keep in mind that parents of multiples tend to use their strollers a bit longer, and are generally tougher on them than parents of singletons, due to longer use. Because you will eventually be pushing lots of weight, look for a stroller that is built to last. At double and triple the prices of single strollers, you won't want to "step up" to another one! *NOTE: Weight limitations are a good indication of sturdiness and the number of years you will be able to make use of the stroller, so compare weight limits before you make your purchase. A sturdy stroller should have a weight limit of at least 38 pounds per seat (per child) or more.*

• • •

Although parents of multiples tend to use their strollers longer, this doesn't necessarily mean they use them more often. Some find they rarely use their strollers due to the physical difficulties of getting everyone out and about (especially those with triplets). If you think you might not use your stroller very often, or if price is a concern, be careful not to spend too much for one!

• • •

If you are pinching pennies and plan to buy a second-hand stroller, make a valiant effort to shop for one locally before you search online. This will save you shipping costs, and will give you an opportunity to look over the stroller before you buy it. If you buy one online, shipping charges may be very costly, and you never really know what you're getting until it's dropped on your doorstep. A friend of mine was so excited to find a Peg Perego stroller for $85 on eBay. Her excitement fizzled when it arrived with a broken foot rest and stained seats, none of which were shown in the photo she saw before placing her bid. If you have no luck locally and want to take your chances shopping online, you can find used strollers in the classified sections of *www.tripletconnection.org*, *www.mostonline.org*, *www.tobuytwo.com*, or *www.ebay.com*.

• • •

Think about spending more on a higher-end model if you can afford it. Higher-end strollers tend to be very durable, easier to maneuver, have more features, and have better resale values (but be careful because some can be heavier than average, due to their quality). Something else to consider: Makers of some higher-end strollers introduce new models every year and often come out with them in the late summer or fall of the previous year (just like car manufacturers do). If new strollers are due to come out on the market soon, you may want to delay your purchase to buy the latest model. Or, if you love the style of a current model you are thinking about, snatch it up quickly before supplies run out!

• • •

If you're tall, do your best to find a stroller with a height-adjustable handle bar (most often a feature on higher-end models). There is nothing worse than looking (and feeling) like the Hunchback of Notre Dame whenever you venture out with your stroller. Trust me, at 5'11," I've had my fill of feeling like Quasimodo! Also, if you are petite, steer clear of strollers that are larger or heavier than average. Any stroller with a weight greater than 35 pounds is quite heavy!

• • •

Realize that having twins does not necessarily mean you should buy a double stroller. You can use a double, two singles, or even a triple if you have other young children in your family. Also, having triplets does not necessarily mean you should buy a triple stroller. Another option, which some choose, is a double and single combination. They are easier to handle, but for obvious reasons, require two people. One major advantage of having a stroller to carry all of your children is that it gives you the freedom to venture out alone. For this reason, most parents buy double or triple strollers to hold both/all of their babies. Consider your lifestyle and what might work best for you and your family before making a decision. *NOTE: Along with a double or triple stroller, you might want to consider a lightweight single stroller for one-on-one time. There are also stroller connectors available that can easily turn two single umbrella strollers into a side-by-side double. You can find them online at* www.greatbabyproducts.com. *(Retail price: $11.95)*

• • •

E-How *(www.ehow.com)* will give you a few more pointers on how to select a good double or triple stroller. They will also give you step-by-step directions on how to do just about anything, including how to change a diaper! Just search for whatever it is you want to learn "how" to do.

• • •

Strollers are a big investment and can be very costly if you end up with a stroller that is not right for you. Just keep in mind that there is no stroller designed for mall shopping, neighborhood strolling, serious running, traveling *and* hiking! Do your research, ask lots of questions, and be sure to shop around for the best price.

• • •

Stroller Accessories:
Consider a few accessories for your stroller, and if any of them are important to you, check to make sure the stroller either comes with the accessory, is offered as an option, or if the stroller can accommodate

the accessory. *NOTE: Many accessories are sold separately, and those marked with a "♥" are what I consider to be great conveniences.*

• • •

Some popular stroller accessories are (check those that are important to you):

_____ Bassinets

_____ Booster seat attachment — for an older child (toddler age)

_____ Bug canopy/net

_____ Belly bar

♥ _____ Double car seat adapters — only a few strollers offer this

_____ Cooler bag

_____ Coordinating diaper bag

♥ _____ Drink holder — for parents

_____ Foot muffs

_____ Junior rider attachment — allows additional child to stand in back

_____ Sicily Double Stroller console by Carry You *(www.carry you.com)*. This product is specially built for side-by-side double strollers and with it you will have plenty of space to organize your cell phone, cups, bottles, keys, wallet, toys and more.

_____ Snack trays

♥ _____ Stroller inserts (snuzzlers) — cradles, and provides support for newborns' heads

_____ Stroller carry bag — for traveling

_____ Sun canopies

_____ Swiss Strolli Rider *(www.happystroller.com)* — bike-like trailer seat for an older child

_____ Tire pump

♥ _____ Mommy Hook *(www.themommyhook.com)*. For $5, this is the greatest invention for mothers with no free hands. This simple hook attaches to any stroller handle bar and carries all sorts of things, including diaper bags, shopping bags, purses, and more.

_____ Umbrella

_____ Weather canopy — additional protection from wind and rain

• • •

Other Modes of Transportation:

Wagons are very popular with parents once their children are old enough to sit unsupported. If you buy one, don't plan to use it in place of a stroller! Wagons are great fun for brief walks, but unlike strollers, children can climb out of them. If you use a wagon beyond your immediate neighborhood, prepare to end up carrying your children and dragging the wagon by your teeth on the return trip!

• • •

Many families end up with a wagon they rarely use because their children don't fit comfortably. If you have twins, shop for a wagon built for two: Radio Flyer has a Voyager Canopy Wagon, Navigator Wagon, and a Pathfinder Wagon. Fisher Price offers a Kid Utility Vehicle that looks like a cross between a stroller and a wagon, and Step 2 has a Safari Wagon, a Wagon for Two, and a T3 Traveler that also looks like a cross between a wagon and stroller. If you have triplets, shop for a wagon built for three: The Step 2 Choo Choo Wagon *and* Choo Choo Trailer, or the Trav-ler Wagon *and* Wagon Trailer by Radio Flyer.

For more information about wagons, call or visit these websites:

Specialty Wagons:
Fisher Price — *www.fisher-price.com* — (800) 432-5437
Step 2 — *www.step2.com* — (800) 347-8372
Radio Flyer — *www.radioflyer.com* — (800) 621-7613

"There is no such thing as a 'perfect' stroller. You will need to consider the features of each style and determine what is best for you and your family. Because of this, it is not uncommon for parents to own two different strollers."
— Beth D. (Mother of 20-month-old GG twins)

"Finding the perfect double stroller is like finding the perfect man – neither exists!"
— Elizabeth B. (Mother of nine children, including twin foster children)

CAR SEAT SAFETY AND TIPS

A car seat can save a child's life, but only if used and installed properly. According to the National Highway Traffic Safety Administration (NHTSA), four out of five car seats are used incorrectly in the United States! Take time to educate yourself about car seat safety before you put the loves of your life in them. For more information, go to the NHTSA's website, *www.nhtsa.dot.gov* under "child passenger safety."

• • •

The SAFEKIDS Coalition offers the four most common mistakes of improper use of a car seat:

1) The *harness is too loose* (it needs to be adjusted so you can slip only one finger between the baby and the harness). Also, the harness should lie flat, not twisted, and the clip that holds them together should be secured level with your child's shoulders.

2) The *car seat is not secure enough to the vehicle* (the safety belt holding the car seat in place should have no more than one inch of movement).

3) *Infants face front too soon* (they should be about one year of age *and* at least 20 pounds).

4) *Children don't use car seats long enough* (a car seat with a full harness until 40 pounds; a seat belt with a booster until 4'9" *and* at least 80 pounds).

• • •

If you want assurance that you have properly installed your car seats and that you are safely strapping your children into them, visit *www.seatcheck.com* or call 1-866-SEAT-CHECK for a car seat inspection station near you. *NOTE: If your babies leave the hospital weighing fewer than five pounds, ask your neonatal team to advise you on how to properly transport them. Many infant car seats are not designed to safely transport premature babies, or those with breathing difficulties.*

• • •

Never buy second hand car seats. There are too may potential dangers associated with them. Some have been recalled, in accidents, or are simply not the safest on the market. Bargains may be difficult to pass up, especially if you see a sign that says "CAR SEATS $10" at a mothers of multiples sale. The offer is even more tempting when the seats appear to be in good condition and there are two or three of them that match. Don't let a bargain sway you into making a wrong decision. Buy new and get the safest car seats for your children.

• • •

There are currently three categories of car seats on the market:

Infant — (birth to 20–22 pounds)
Convertible — (birth to 40 pounds)
Booster — (40–80 pounds)

• • •

Don't make the mistake of buying "convertible" instead of "infant" car seats. Although the convertible accommodates infants as well as older babies, the infant seats are well worth the added expense for the following reasons:

• They are safer for infants because they are a better fit.

- Your babies will probably be smaller than average and will use them for a longer period of time.
- They are often used as infant carriers, which can be very convenient.
- When babies fall asleep, you won't have to disturb them when taking them out of the car, because the seats pop out of the base.
- Some strollers have adapters that can accommodate two infant car seats.
- Infant seats can also be used to feed multiples.

Buy the infant car seat, then the convertible, and finally, the booster.

• • •

Helpful hint: Decide which stroller you want *before* you buy car seats. I can't tell you how many people I know who have returned their car seats because the stroller they bought had car seat adapters that did not fit the car seats they purchased. The following is a listing of double strollers that accommodate two infant car seats. If you plan to buy one of these strollers, make sure you buy compatible infant car seats. If the car seats are not listed on the website, call the customer service number to find out:

Stroller	Manufacturer	Customer Service
Big Caboose	www.joovy.com	(877) 456-5049
Double Decker	www.doubledeckerstroller.com	(239) 543-1582
Duette SW	www.pegperego.com	(800) 671-1701
Duo Glider	www.gracobaby.com	(800) 345-4109
Rock & Roll	www.bergdesign.net	(800) 832-2376
Safety 1st	www.safety1st.com	(800) 544-1108
Snap 'N Go (cannot be used beyond 12 months)	www.babytrend.com	(562) 949-8607
Spider Duo (adapter sold separately)	www.stroll-air.com	(519) 579-4534

Strollers that accommodate three infant car seats are:

Stroller	Manufacturer	Customer Service
Rock & Roll	www.bergdesign.net	(800) 832-2376
Triple Decker	www.doubledecker.com	(239) 543-1582
Triplette SW	www.pegperego.com	(800) 671-1701

THE POOP ON DIAPERS (AND WIPES)

Much thought has been given to "guesstimate" just how many diapers a typical baby will use in a day. My theory is that the amount of diapers a child uses has much to do with parents. Parents of singletons tend to change diapers more often, whereas parents of multiples generally change diapers "as soon as they can" or when it can no longer be avoided! Most moms of multiples I have talked to estimate that they use about 10 diapers a day, or 70 per week per child (this is their "generous" estimate). Expect this to be a good approximation of the number of diapers you will use per week *per child* during the infant stage.

• • •

Don't take diapers out of their packages until you are confident you will use them. The reality is no one really knows the exact number of each size your babies will need when they are first born.

• • •

If you assume you will be changing your twin newborns 10 times a day, a large pack of diapers (68 count) will last just about 3½ days. If you have triplets, the pack should last about two days. *NOTE: When you shop, look for a sale, stock up, and bring someone with you to help carry your piles of Pampers out of the store.*

· · ·

You will be changing many more diapers in the infant stage than any other. The average of 10 diapers you change per day per child will gradually decrease to about five or six by the time your children become toddlers. *NOTE: Although the amount of time you spend changing diapers will decrease, don't expect to save any money! The larger the diaper, the more expensive it becomes:*

DIAPERS		PAMPERS/ HUGGIES Wholesale Club	PAMPERS/ HUGGIES Grocery Store	LUVS Grocery Store
Size	Weight			
1–2	Up to 15 lbs	15¢	19¢	16¢
3	16–28 lbs	17¢	23¢	19¢
4	22–37 lbs	20¢	26¢	22¢
5	27–36 lbs	22¢	30¢	25¢
6	over 36 lbs	27¢	40¢	32¢

· · ·

Save money by buying the smallest diapers you can, without them being uncomfortable for your children. Also, avoid buying specialty diapers, like "premium" or "supreme" unless you really need them (sleep training and long trips are examples of when you might want to use them). Premium diapers have premium price tags, and are not an every day necessity.

· · ·

Do some browsing and have a good idea where to go to get the best price for diapers before your supply runs out. This will save you time and money once you start needing them by the truckload. Brand, where you choose to shop, and the distance you travel to shop for them will affect the price. As a general rule, the best place to shop for diapers is wholesale stores, such as Costco or Sam's Club, for both brand-name and generic diapers. Wal-Mart, K-Mart and Target are also reasonable. *NOTE: When you shop for diapers, buy them by the case. Cases of diapers are cheaper and easier to stack and store in a closet or pantry.*

• • •

When price is not much of an issue, most mothers reach for Huggies and Pampers diapers. It may also help to know that Luvs brand diapers are of good quality and quite a bit cheaper in price (they are made by the same company that makes Pampers). I have tried a number of brands, including generic, and have yet to find a diaper that doesn't serve its purpose (although I found the brands mentioned to be the best overall). Some are a bit softer or more absorbent, others are slightly better fitting, and others seem to be a bit more comfortable for babies. When buying diapers, you will probably end up with a specific brand, not because of quality, but because of its price, and your budget.

• • •

Here is an interesting price comparison for "Size 1" diapers (based on grocery store prices):

Huggies and Pampers = 19¢ per diaper

Luvs = 16¢ per diaper

If you use Luvs diapers, diapering twins in the first year equates to about $218 in savings and about $329 if you have triplets.

• • •

If you are pinching pennies, shop for a generic brand of diapers. Generic brands can save you as much as 25–30% over name brands. The savings (assuming 25%) over a three-year period will be about $1,050 with twins, and $1,575 with triplets! *NOTE: Remember, the savings per diaper becomes more significant as diapers get larger and more expensive.*

• • •

If you use name-brand diapers, plan to spend about $4,161 for twins and $6,241 for triplets. Using generic diapers, you will spend about $3,113 (twins) and $4,669 (triplets). Expect to change about 16,060 diapers if you have twins, and 24,090 diapers with triplets by the time your multiples are potty trained!

• • •

Other "must-haves" that add to the cost of each and every diaper change are baby wipes. There are several varieties ranging from generic to supreme, and all serve the same purpose, except some are better than others! Although they are more expensive, most parents prefer Huggies, Pampers, and Playtex Baby Magic wipes. They are the softest, thickest wipes on the market, and although other brands are cheaper and offer more wipes per box, you will end up using more wipes per diaper change because they are thin and lack moisture. Don't skimp on baby wipes. At the end of the day, you won't save any money. *NOTE: Luvs baby wipes are fairly new on the market, and are also becoming popular.*

• • •

The best way to save money on wipes is not by brand, but *packaging* and *quantity*. If you buy a single container of "name brand" baby wipes, expect to spend about 4 cents per wipe (times two or three baby butts...that's at least 8–12 cents per round of diaper changes!). If you buy wipes by the case, or *large* refill bags, the cost is cut in half to about 2 cents per wipe. *NOTE: If you shop at Costco, look for Kirkland Signature baby wipes by the case. They are the least expensive wipes around, and although they are not quite as absorbent and soft as the name brands, in my opinion, they are a good enough quality for the price.*

• • •

Many new mothers prefer to make their own baby wipes in an effort to save money. If you have an interest in trying the following recipe, remember to double it. Your wipes won't last long with multiples!

Homemade Baby Wipes

Cut one roll of strong paper towels in half (Brawny or Bounty work well).
NOTE: When you cut the towels, stand them up vertically and cut across the towels in the center, creating a top and bottom.

Mix together in a bowl:
1 Cup warm water
1 Tablespoon baby bath soap
1 Tablespoon baby oil

Place half the roll of paper towels in an empty baby wipe container.
Pour the liquid mixture over the towels.
Remove cardboard tube (it should pull right out).
After cooling, pull towels from the center of the roll.

"Strong enough for a man...but made for a baby."
— A consumer review of Pampers baby wipes

THE LOW DOWN ON HIGHCHAIRS

It's best to wait until your babies are ready to use highchairs before you purchase them. You will want to keep your money in the bank as long as possible (prices range between $60 and $250), and they will crowd your kitchen no matter how many double ovens or islands it has.

• • •

Consider secondhand highchairs. They can be found in your sister's basement, your brother's attic, and also at church rummage, garage, and mothers of multiples tag sales in good condition for a fraction of their retail price.

• • •

Think again before buying highchairs with solid white seat covers. I bought all-white highchairs thinking they would match my kitchen; what a decorating faux-pas that turned out to be! White highchairs always look dirty, no matter how clean they are, so look for a pattern to hide the dirt and save the interior decorating for later!

• • •

After a number of meals are served, your highchairs will require some heavy duty cleaning. Because they are impossible to fully clean with a sponge, you will eventually need to think of more creative ways to wash them. One way is to take them outdoors and hose and scrub them down with soap and water. If you can, take the seat covers off when you do this. You will need to remove the buffet of food that you find under-neath. Another solution is to give your highchairs a hot shower. Showers work wonders at making highchairs look and feel clean and refreshed!

• • •

Expect to spend a ridiculous amount of time cleaning highchairs on a daily basis. The worst part about them is that you will have more than one, and cleaning them will become one of your biggest frustrations and time-wasters. The sooner you can get your children to sit at a table, the better. Getting rid of highchairs means less work for you!

• • •

The good news is there are alternatives highchairs. Here are a few sug-gestions (for the short term):

1) Feed your babies in the most upright position in their infant car seats for as long as you can.
2) Purchase Bebe Pods *(www.bebepod.com)* or Bumbo Seats *(www.bumboseat.com)* and feed them in these seats (for babies ages 3–12 months). *(Retail price: $35)*
3) Buy a large floor mat and have picnics on the kitchen floor whenever possible.

• • •

Another alternative to highchairs is a "daycare table." Don't think you run a daycare facility? Actually, you do, you just don't get paid for your hard work or have a staff of people to help you. Daycare tables (also known as "toddler tables," or "twin or triplet tables") are much easier to clean, less mess on the floor, and they also serve as an activity table. I bought one secondhand because I got tired of cleaning highchairs. When I made the switch, I regretted not having one from the very beginning. They accom-modate children ages five months to 24 months (+). You can find these tables for twins, triplets or more by visiting *www.justmultiples.com.* *NOTE: Make sure you have enough space in your kitchen before you order one. Unlike highchairs, the table is one unit and does not fold up.*

• • •

If space in your kitchen is a real concern, you may want to stick with highchairs and buy Space Saver Highchairs by Fisher-Price. These strap securely onto your kitchen chairs, and they convert into booster seats. You can find them online at *www.fisher-price.com*.

MINIVANS AND OTHER MINUTIAE

With multiples on the way, I am sure you have said at least once, "I *refuse* to drive a minivan!" If not, then perhaps you said, "I will not be caught *dead* in a minivan!" If you are considering some other form of transportation, that is fine. Just realize that you will be in a small minority among mothers with young multiples. Minivans are not quite as common with mothers of twins, although most I know (with kids under five years) drive one, and every mother I know with triplets cruises around in one (except one who drives a station wagon).

• • •

Some food for thought: When it comes to transporting twins or triplets, your first priority should be safety; your next priority should be convenience, the next, convenience, and the next, convenience! You will soon find out that nothing else matters. The fact is there is no other mode of transportation more convenient than a minivan for parents with multiple young children.

• • •

If you are in the market for a new (or different) form of transportation, look to the following websites for photos, specs, prices, and reviews:

> *www.autobytel.com*
> *www.automotive.com*
> *www.minivansearch.com* — *(Go ahead...take a look!)*
> *www.vehix.com*

• • •

Once you review these websites, you should have a good idea of what makes and models interest you. Just make sure you don't limit your list based on looks and price alone. Let's face it, our teenage years are over! With children, and more than one to drive around, you will need to consider other features that may not be so attractive, but more practical for your family.

• • •

Before you make any decisions about buying a new vehicle or keeping the one you have, visit the National Highway Traffic Safety Administration's "Safer Car" website *(www.safercar.gov)* for details on crash test and rollover results for new cars, and cars dating back to 1990. This site is very informative!

• • •

While shopping, don't forget that you will need to transport not only your babies, but all the "stuff" that goes along with them. Even if you plan to have a quick lunch at Grandma's house, packing everyone up will be much like going on vacation for a month! Visiting Grandma will require organization, half the contents of your house, and enough space in your vehicle. Remember, if you go out as a family, most often the entire back of your vehicle will be taken over by children and a stroller. Where will you put everything else if aren't driving a minivan (or SUV)? Do you want to make two or three trips to the baby superstore every week, or one? This will depend on the vehicle you are driving.

• • •

You might ask, "Why not a large Sport Utility Vehicle?" SUVs are certainly spacious, and will serve the purpose, but they are not as practical for the following reasons:

MINIVANS vs. SUVS	
MINIVANS — Advantages	**SUVS — Advantages**
More fuel efficient	Some seat more passengers
Better rollover rating	More cargo capacity in back — larger models
On average, not as expensive	Considered a bit more "stylish"
Better access to children (while inside the vehicle)	
Easier to lift children in and out (vehicle is not as high off the ground)	
Parents can move about the vehicle (in models with no front console)	
Easier to park, as a result, often not as far to walk	
Many offer automatic door openers (both sides and trunk)	
Some have captains chairs (that can be easily removed, if necessary)	
Overall, much more "family friendly"	
Better suited for your new "Twins/Triplets On Board" bumper sticker!	

• • •

The following is a list of important features to keep in mind while shopping for a vehicle:

Vehicle Shopping List:

GOOD CRASH TEST AND ROLLOVER RATING — Make sure you do your fact-finding beforehand and shop for one of the safest! *NOTE: Visit* www.safercar.gov *for details.*

• • •

REVIEW CONSUMER FEEDBACK — Buy a vehicle that others have tried, tested and like. Chances are if most consumers are happy with their purchase, you will be too.

• • •

ON-STAR SERVICES — Many newer (General Motors) vehicles offer On-Star services. This is a safety feature which you can subscribe to that can possibly save a life if you are in a serious accident, or if some other problem arises while driving. On-Star can also track the scene of your accident and send help to your location without delay, even if you are unable to call or speak. On-Star also offers roadside assistance, a remote door unlock system, a phone calling feature, and other services. Visit *www.onstar.com* to learn more. *NOTE: This is a service available for General Motors vehicles.*

• • •

AAA MEMBERSHIP — A subscription that offers various services that don't seem like much, until you need them. These include tire changes, jumps, new batteries, and other services. Their membership also offers discounts on certain car rentals, hotels, and more. *NOTE: I have called on them a few times, and each time they came to my rescue within 10–20 minutes.*

• • •

CAPTAIN'S CHAIRS — If you buy a minivan, look for one with removable captain's chairs (bucket seats) in the center and a bench in the back. With captain's chairs, one (or both) chairs can be removed for extra cargo space for all those bulky purchases you will soon be making. If you find you don't use one of the chairs on a regular basis, remove it until someone needs it. Removing a seat offers easy access to your babies while inside the vehicle, and also makes it easier to get them in and out.

• • •

ROOF RACK — Don't forget about the stroller that will take up all of the space in the back. Unlike most, you might someday use a roof rack!

• • •

WINDOW SHADES (?) — Buy at least two if your vehicle does not have tinted windows.

• • •

AUTOMATIC DOOR OPENER — A very convenient feature in minivans for parents who have no spare hands. I am convinced the person who invented this is a parent of multiples. If not, he or she is a genius (with lots of kids).

• • •

ADDITIONAL STORAGE IN FLOOR — Some new vehicles offer additional storage in the floor. This is great for storing extra diapers, wipes, clothing and other supplies that you don't necessarily need on a daily basis, but should have on hand, just in case.

• • •

TV/MOVIE SCREEN (?) — In a nutshell, "You're damned if you do, and damned if you don't" have one installed. I have one, and I must admit that I hate to love it. I really hesitate to offer my opinion about these, but here goes: Consider the fact that your babies will be facing backward in their car seats for the first year of their lives. In other words, they won't be "watching" anything in the car (other than the fabric on the seat they are facing) for quite some time. Keep this in mind, and consider having one installed only if you take frequent, longer trips, because it will eventually come in handy. If not, save your money until your next vehicle purchase, then go for it!

• • •

LEATHER INTERIOR (?) — Think about spending a few extra dollars for leather interior. Leather, as opposed to fabric, is very easy to clean and has a better resale value. *NOTE: If you live in a very warm climate, fabric material may be a better option, because leather can become very hot.*

• • •

RUBBER FLOOR MATS — Rubber floor mats are much easier to keep clean than standard floor mats because you can hose them down. If they are sold as an option, opt for them.

• • •

CHILD SAFETY LOCKS — Before you buy a vehicle (especially a second hand one), make sure it comes with child safety locks and that they are engaged as soon as you drive it home. *NOTE: I drove around for months with my new minivan before I realized the safety locks were never engaged! Make sure you put yours to use right away.*

• • •

CUP HOLDERS — Confirm that there are cup holders for every seat, or at least most of them.

• • •

FRONT AND SIDE AIR BAGS — For obvious reasons, the more air bags, the better.

• • •

TINTED WINDOWS — Just about all new cars now have tinted windows, but check, just to be sure (especially if you are looking for a used car). It's tough to get kids to sleep or rest if too much light comes into the car.

• • •

MAKE SURE YOUR VEHICLE IS BIG ENOUGH! — Don't try to squeeze two (or three) car seats into a car that is too small for your family. Save the convertible sports car for later! *NOTE: There are many cars that will not fit two or more infant car seats across the back seat. If you plan to use a standard car or SUV with one back seat, be sure to measure the width (from inside, with the doors closed). Take this measurement with you when you purchase car seats to confirm that they will fit.*

• • •

Auto Accessories:
FIRST AID KIT — Keep one in your vehicle at all times.

• • •

INFANT VIEW CAR MIRROR — Allows Mom to have eyes in the back of her head. These are a safe way to monitor your little ones while driving. *NOTE: Look for the 2-in-1 Wide Angle Mirror by One Step Ahead (www.onestepahead.com). (Retail price: $14.95) It's easy to mount in both forward and rear facing positions (although this product will not work well for babies in the far back seat).*

• • •

TISSUES — Keep a large box in your vehicle. Someone is always sneezing, spitting up, or crying!

• • •

EXTRA DIAPERS AND WIPES — Always keep an extra supply of diapers and wipes in your car, because you *will* use them. Replace them when your supply runs low.

• • •

EXTRA CLOTHING (FOR MOM AND BABIES) — Keep one complete change of baby clothing and an extra shirt for Mom in the car.

• • •

EXTRA POWDERED FORMULA — If you bottle feed, carry an extra container of powdered formula (and a spare bottle) in the car. When you need to feed someone while traveling, all you will need is water. *NOTE: Look for Sassy's Powdered Formula Dispenser (www.sassybaby.com).*

...

EXTRA SET OF KEYS — Keep a single spare car and house key in your wallet (or bottom of your purse) just in case.

...

RESEALABLE PLASTIC BAGS — Perfect for dirty diapers and clothing you end up with on the go.

...

BACK-OF-SEAT CAR ORGANIZER — Buy at least one for the back of your seats. It will help to keep the interior a bit more organized and uncluttered. *NOTE: Look for either the Trios Tote 3-in-1 Organizer, or the jumbo Safe-Fit Backseat Valet. Both are available at* www.onestepahead.com. *(Retail price: $16.95)*

...

GARBAGE "CAN" — Look for the "Floor Trash Stand" by One Step Ahead *(www.onestepahead.com)*. (Retail price: $13.95) It's safe, waterproof, and won't tip.

...

A FEW AGE APPROPRIATE TOYS — For entertainment on the go.

...

AIR FRESHENER — Perfect for hiding unpleasant smells. A friend of mine suggested one of these after she sat in my car and asked, "What stinks?" I thought my minivan smelled just fine, but apparently this was not the case!

...

A MAP — You won't want to get lost with multiples in the back seat! *NOTE: If you use a more elaborate GPS (Global Positioning Satellite) system, make sure the computerized voice is loud enough to talk over the babies. If it's not at least as loud as a dull roar, you will probably not be able to hear the directions! Save hundreds by sticking with a good old-fashioned map if this is the case.*

...

If you are looking to save money, and lots of it, purchase a previously leased or low-mileage vehicle. Imagine the diapers or frivolous outfits you can buy with the savings!

• • •

Bring your calculator if you are thinking about leasing versus buying a vehicle. Many leases seem like a better deal on paper if you look at them on a monthly basis. The reality is many lease options turn out to be more expensive if you compare the total cost of the lease to an outright purchase. This is not always the case, but it is certainly worth your time to do that math.

• • •

Before you lease or buy a vehicle, it might be worth your while to rent (for a week or two) the make and model you are considering. This will enable you to make sure it will serve its "multiple" purposes, and that everyone and everything fits.

THINGS THAT DON'T COST ANYTHING

There are freebies you can request from manufacturers marketing to new parents of twins or more. Most companies require a letter stating that you are requesting a freebie, your name, shipping information, e-mail address, and a copy of a birth certificate for each child.

• • •

The following is a sample letter that you can use when drafting your letters:

Date

Company Name
Address
RE: *Multiple Birth Program*

Dear Sir or Madam,

On (birth date), my husband and I became the proud parents of (twins/ triplets). We understand that your company offers promotional products (or coupons) to families with multiples. We would like to take advantage of this offer. Enclosed are copies of birth certificates for our children.

Thank you for your time, consideration, and support. We greatly appreciate it!

Sincerely,

Name
Address
Phone
E-mail

• • •

The following is a list of companies that currently offer multiple birth promotions:
NOTE: This list is not all-inclusive.

Baby's First Circus Program
Field Entertainment, Inc.
8607 Westwood Center Drive
Vienna, VA 22182
www.ringling.com/offers/baby.aspx
Free ticket for each child to use any time during lifetime — Ringling Brothers Barnum & Bailey Circus

Beechnut Food Corporation
Checker Board Square
St. Louis, MO 63164
(800) 523-6633
www.beech-nut.com
Promotional packet and coupons

Drypers Corporation
ATTN: Multiple Birth Program
P.O. Box 8830
Vancouver, WA 98666
(360) 693-6688
www.drypers.com
Coupons for free package of diapers for each baby

Earth's Best Baby Food
(800) 442-4221
www.earthsbest.com
Coupons

Evenflo Products
Multiple Birth Program
1801 Commerce Drive
Piqua, OH 45356
(800) 356-2229
www.evenflo.com
Disposable bottles, nipples, and sippy cups

Fisher-Price
(800) 432-5437
www.fisher-price.com
Brochures, catalogs, coupons

Gerber
Multiple Birth Program
445 State Street
Fremont, MI 49413
(800) 4-GERBER
www.gerber.com
Quarterly magazine with coupons, feeding spoons

Heinz Baby Food
(800) 872-2229
www.heinzbaby.com
Booklet, coupons

Johnson & Johnson Consumer Products, Inc.
199 Grandview Road
Skillman, NJ 08558
(800) 526-3967
www.johnsonsbaby.com
Brochures, coupons, samples

Kimberly-Clark Corporation (Huggies)
Multiple Birth Program
Department QMB
P.O. Box 2020
Neenah, WI 54957
(800) 544-1847
www.huggies.com
Coupons and free products

K-Mart
(800) 533-0143
www.kmart.com
Coupons

McNeil Consumer Products (Tylenol)
(800) 962-5357
www.tylenol.com
Coupons

Mead Johnson (Enfamil)
ATTN: Public Affairs Department
2404 Pennsylvania Street
Evansville, IN 47721
(800) 222-9123
www.enfamil.com
One-time shipment of free formula — one case per baby. Also, contact your pediatrician for the Mead Johnson sales representative in your area for promotions and products.

Nestle Infant Nutrition
P.O. Box AW
Wilkes Barre, PA 18703
(800) 284-9488
www.verybestbaby.com
Coupons for free formula

Novartis Pharmaceuticals (Triaminic)
(800) KIDS-987
Samples, coupons

One Step Ahead
(800) 274-8840
www.onestepahead.com
Mail-order catalog; discount for multiples

Perfectly Safe
(800) 837-KIDS
www.perfectlysafe.com
Childproofing catalog; discounts for multiples

Playtex Products
20 Troy Road
Whittany, NJ 07981
(800) 222-0453
www.playtexbaby.com
$7 rebate on purchase of a Diaper Genie

Proctor & Gamble Company (Pampers/Luvs)
Pampers Multiple Birth Program
P.O. Box 599
Cincinnati, OH 45201
(800) 543-0480
www.pampers.com
www.luvs.com
Diapers, coupons, wipes, detergent

Right Start
(800) LITTLE-1
www.rightstart.com
Discount for multiples

Ross Laboratories (Similac)
624 Cleveland Ave.
Columbus, OH 43216
(800) 222-9546
www.similac.com
Welcome Addition Club — Coupons

Scott Paper
(800) 835-7268
www.scottpaper.com
Coupons

Sensational Beginnings
P.O. Box 2099
987 Stewart Road
Monroe, MI 48162
(800) 444-2147
www.sensationalbeginnings.com
Catalog — Educational toys; discounts for multiples

Tiny Love/The Maya Group, Inc.
Multiple Birth Program
12622 Monarch Street
Garden Grove, CA 92841
(888) TINY-LOVE
www.tinylove.com
Buy one/get one free on all Tiny Love products purchased directly through its website (call for more information first)

Toys "R" Us/Babies "R" Us
(800) TOYS-R-US
www.toysrus.com
www.babiesrus.com
Seasonal catalogs w/ coupons — Discount on multiple items of the same product

Twins Magazine
(800) 328-3211
www.twinsmagazine.com
One free issue of *Twins Magazine*

The First Years
One Kiddie Drive
Avon, MA 02322
(800) 533-6708
www.thefirstyears.com
Bibs and rattle for each baby

White House Greetings Office
Room 39
1600 Pennsylvania Ave, N.W.
Washington, DC 20500
Welcome card (or birthday) from the president — need to specify which you would like

• • •

Before you grab a pen and paper and contact every manufacturer under the sun, consider the following:

1) Question which freebies are worth your time and the stamp.
2) You can (and should) get started on this as soon as possible. Work on your letter and address envelopes before your babies arrive, but realize that most companies won't send anything unless you provide copies of the birth certificates.
3) Companies may change their freebies and policies. You might get a "Dear Jane" letter back saying, "Congratulations!" and that's it. Some are now moving toward offering freebies to families of higher order multiples (triplets and more).
4) Don't expect to get anything of great value, like a free minivan, or lifetime supply of diapers. You will need to give birth to many more babies in order to take advantage of this!

• • •

Whether you are expecting twins or octuplets, diaper manufacturers are worth contacting. When you get in touch with them, you will receive coupons and will be on their mailing list for future promotions. Some companies to contact are:

Pampers — *www.pampers.com* — (800) PAMPERS
Huggies — *www.huggies.com* — (888) 525-8388
Luvs — *www.luvs.com* — (888) NO-LEAKS

• • •

Register online with Gerber *(www.gerber.com)* and Beech-Nut *(www.beechnut.com)* and get free monthly e-newsletters on nutrition, parenting, and feeding tips. They also offer coupons to those who register, and occasionally send free samples in the mail. Yum!

• • •

Ask your pediatrician for baby formula whenever you visit. Pediatricians often get stockpiles of it from their formula reps and while the amount you get may not be much relative to what you need, every bit will help! Don't forget to ask for samples of over-the-counter of medications as well.

• • •

For other cyberspace coupons and more information regarding freebies, visit the following websites:

www.babycenter.com/freestuff/
www.babychatter.com
*www.momsview.com
www.preemietwins.com/twinsfreestuff.htm
www.totaldeals.com
www.twinslist.org/freebie.htm

*NOTE: Moms View (www.momsview.com) *offers an overview of hundreds of free products available to all families. They also have Babies "R" Us promotion codes, printable coupons, and multiple birth coupons.*

ORGANIZING AND CREATING SPACE

Without going crazy, get your house in order as best as you can. One of the best ways to stay organized after your babies are born is to organize as much as possible before they are born. Clean and get rid of as much "stuff" as you possibly can (or better yet, ask your husband to do it). Look to *www.organizedhome.com* for some helpful hints.

• • •

Designate a cabinet in your kitchen for storing baby supplies. Find a large space that is easy to reach and has at least one shelf per baby. You should also designate a large drawer for kids' only items, such as spill-proof cup tops, pacifiers, and bottle nipples. Using baskets to store these things will only clutter countertops.

• • •

Consider purchasing a second refrigerator or freezer, especially if you have other children. Mothers of multiples often complain about lack of space in their refrigerators. A friend of mine once told me that her neighbor (a new mother of twins) showed up at her house one day with a bag. She thought she was offering a gift until she asked, "Would you mind storing some of my breast milk in your freezer?" If you find yourself using a neighbor's freezer, it might be time for a second refrigerator! Before you buy one, clean and organize the one you have. You might find that you have space, and plenty of it.

• • •

Put a spare dresser to good use. If it has drawers in it, use it to store a few changes of your babies' clothing and put it on the first floor of your home. If you relocate a spare dresser, you will save yourself lots of steps and create more storage space.

• • •

Buy a large attractive trunk (with rounded edges) that will look nice in your family room. You will need a place to toss toys, and something that looks nice is always better than a toy box that looks like a big plastic storage container.

• • •

Use the space under cribs to store bulky possessions including blankets, large toys, memorabilia boxes, and other items. Once you add cribs to a nursery, you will find that there isn't much space left other than the space under cribs. Make use of it.

• • •

Since chances are good your multiples will be sharing a bedroom, at least initially, you can install a second rack for hanging additional clothing in a nursery closet. You might have to raise an existing rack in order to create more room for another rack underneath. Nevertheless, it is very simple to do.

• • •

For more elaborate storage options, Hold Everything is worth checking into *(www.holdeverything.com)*, as well as California Closets *(www.californiaclosets.com)*. The folks at California Closets will come out and do all of the work for you for a few hundred dollars. This might sound expensive, but you might want to consider doing this instead of spending hundreds on a dresser.

• • •

Look for a vertical shoe rack that hangs from a rack in your babies' closet. This keeps shoes organized and off the floor.

•••

If you have a basement, consider creating closet space for extra storage. When clothing and lack of space begin to grow exponentially, you might find your basement to be your best storage option.

•••

Before you think about moving due to lack of space in your home, consider adding raised or racked shelving in your garage. This is bound to be a cheaper alternative to shopping for a new house!

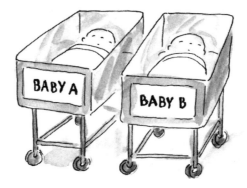

BABY A BABY B

THE MULTIPLE BIRTH

Ask your doctor how long he or she expects your stay in the hospital to be and plan accordingly (this varies from state to state). Most mothers expecting twins and triplets end up having a cesarean birth, whether they plan to or not. Since this is the case, it's better to pack too much than not enough.

· · ·

When you pack to go to the hospital, what you will need is no different from what any other expectant mother would need. However, you should pack two (or three) going home outfits (one for each child), and high-waisted underwear to avoid the incision from your more-than-likely cesarean birth.

· · ·

Unlike most new mothers of singletons, those with multiples often end up being discharged from the hospital before their newborns. As a general rule, if you are beyond 34 weeks gestation, it's probably a good idea to pack clothing for your babies (but this is not a guarantee that you will use them). If you are less than 34 weeks along, there is a good chance you will be released from the hospital before your babies and packing outfits for them will not be necessary.

• • •

If needed, some baby essentials (per child) to bring with you to the hospital should include:

1 comfortable outfit
1 warm blanket
1 receiving blanket
1 infant car seat
1 head rest (car seat insert)

NOTE: The hospital should provide other essentials for the trip home, including diapers, bottled formula, an infant hat, and a few toiletries.

• • •

You will need one car seat for each baby if they both/all leave the hospital with you. However, whether they come home with your or not, it's a good idea to install car seats a few weeks before your "anticipated" due date and be sure to follow the manufacturer's directions for proper installation.

• • •

Since hospital beds aren't comfortable for very long, bring your favorite blanket and pillow from home. You will want to be as comfortable as possible, both before and after the delivery. Having the "comforts of home" will help you to get as much rest as you can.

• • •

Some other items you might want to take with you to the hospital:

- Insurance cards and policy numbers
- Pediatrician's name, address and phone number
- Video camera and charger
- Snacks
- Slippers
- Money
- Camera
- Film
- Batteries
- Robe
- Chapstick

- Thick socks (no matter what the season — hospitals can be very cold at night)
- Snug bra (or nursing bra)
- Nursing pillow (if you already have one, otherwise use regular pillows)
- Toiletries (toothbrush, paste, soap, shampoo, conditioner, deodorant, lotion)
- Hospital contact list
- Baby name book
- Pen and paper
- Comfortable going home outfit (plan to be in maternity wear)
- Pajamas (button-down if you plan to nurse)
- High-waisted underwear
- Hair clips or ties
- Makeup (if you so desire)
- Small hand-held mirror
- Hairbrush/comb
- Personal address book
- Favorite magazines
- Baby books (for first footprints)
- Large bag (to carry gifts home)

• • •

Many new mothers of premature infants are somewhat relieved when they are discharged from the hospital before their babies. Going home first offers new moms a chance to regroup, recuperate and to get some much-needed sleep before their babies come home. If your babies spend any time in the hospital after you are discharged, take advantage of every moment possible to rest and recuperate.

• • •

Your babies may not come home from the hospital together. If their discharge times are scattered, you will need to think about who will care for one (or two) infants at home while you visit the other(s) who remain(s) in the hospital. Make arrangements in advance, just in case.

• • •

Those with very premature babies can have an exceptionally difficult and stressful start to motherhood, and unfortunately, get to know the hospital all too well. If your babies are born much earlier than you expected, visit *www.preemietwins.com* for support and more information regarding prematurity. *Preemietwins.com* was created by a mother of twin daughters born thirteen weeks before their due date. You can read about her experience and others, as well as share your own. *NOTE: Other popular preemie websites include* www.preemiecare.org, www.preemieparents.com, *and* www.preemiemagazine.com.

• • •

If you deliver prematurely (before 37 weeks gestation), your babies may spend time in the neonatal intensive care unit (NICU) for observation. Be aware that most hospitals with NICUs restrict visitors to parents and grandparents. If this is your hospital's policy, other family members and friends will not have an opportunity to see your babies during their stay in the NICU. This happened to me, and my not-so-immediate family was very disappointed. Let your family and friends know that this is a possibility before they make plans to visit you and your babies in the hospital.

• • •

If friends and family don't get an opportunity to see your babies in the hospital, ask one of the hospital staff members to take Polaroid (or digital) pictures so friends and family won't have to wait to see your new additions. Many hospitals offer to take pictures for this reason.

• • •

If you have an uneventful pregnancy, consider videotaping the birth. Even if you think you are not interested, take the video camera to the hospital just in case you change your mind. Today, this is the most treasured video I own, as well as my children's favorite video to watch.

• • •

If you deliver by cesarean section in a Level III hospital, expect to have an entourage of people in the operating room. As an example, when I gave birth to triplets, I counted 19 people! This included my new family of 5, but when I did the quick math, I realized there were also 14 medical professionals in attendance. Be prepared, and not overwhelmed by the experience.

• • •

Be prepared for the possibility of giving birth in an operating room regardless of whether you plan to have a cesarean section or vaginal birth. Many doctors prefer this setting given the increased chance of complications that are inherent in a multiple birth.

• • •

Get out of bed and walk (or at a minimum, sit up in a chair) as soon as you can after a cesarean delivery! Ask the nursing staff to wake you as soon as you are allowed to get out of bed, and when they wake you, be sure to get up! I was told to "get out of bed" but chose to sleep instead. When I woke up, I had the worst pain I had ever experienced, not from the surgery, but from gas pain! Everyone's response to a cesarean section is different. However, don't take a chance at having an experience similar to mine. Try to get out of bed as soon as you can to help diminish gas buildup.

· · ·

If practical, your husband might want to consider spreading his vacation time over a period of weeks rather than all at once following the birth. Most often, there is a house full of people lending a helping hand at first, and then they go home. If your husband chooses to scatter his vacation time, you will look forward to your husband's company, and his help, especially after your friends and family leave. *NOTE: Choosing to take two days off a week for several weeks might work well.*

· · ·

When you arrive home from the hospital, turn off your phone's ringer and get some rest: Your phone will ring off the hook with well-wishers who don't have much to say other than "congratulations." Although the calls are intended to congratulate you, they can turn into marathon conversations, especially when you don't have the time or energy to talk for any length of time. Return the calls when you find a time convenient for you.

· · ·

If you feel the need to pick and choose your calls, a phone service with Caller ID can help you to screen calls and save you from unnecessary conversations.

· · ·

Leave updates on the status of the babies on your phone answering machine or simply announce the birth with date, time, names, lengths and weights of each baby. This simple recording will answer the majority of questions callers will have regarding the birth.

· · ·

Send a quick e-mail out to friends and family and attach a picture of your new family members. E-mail is a perfect way to keep in touch with everyone, as well as reduce your phone calls. You might want to add a note that says something like, "We are all doing well and will be in touch as soon we have a chance to get settled."

• • •

Headaches in the first few months following a multiple birth are not uncommon. If the babies' crying doesn't give you one, the interrupted sleep and exhaustion will! Check the stock in your medicine cabinet to make sure you have a sufficient supply of pain reliever on hand.

• • •

Expect to bleed for several weeks following your delivery. Stock up on lots of maxi pads. Your best bet is to go with the longest, thickest size you can find on the store shelf.

• • •

Don't be so quick to donate or lend out your maternity clothing to an expectant friend once you deliver. If you do, you will probably need to ask for them back. Expect to continue to look pregnant for a few months, if not much longer. After giving birth, I managed to squeeze into one of my pre-pregnancy bathing suits while on a vacation one winter. As I walked along the beach holding in my stomach, a woman approached and asked, "When are you due?" When I said, "Seven months ago," I think I taught her a valuable lesson. She also taught me a lesson about wearing a bathing suit that didn't fit!

• • •

If you have stretch marks, get used to them. All of the cocoa butter in the world won't help! If you decide to have a tummy tuck it might help, but you will need a good plastic surgeon, a lot of money, and time to rest after the surgery. If you are like most mothers of multiples, you won't have the latter two after you have given birth!

"If you end up having identical twins don't expect them to be identical.
I have eight-year-old identical twin boys and the only things they have
in common are their looks and their birthday (the 4th of July). I have discovered
over the years that being identical means that each child, regardless of DNA,
is very different, and that concept is often hard to understand.
Being an identical twin is simply having a best friend who looks like you!"
— Kathy S. (Mother of identical twin boys and a daughter)

THE PEDIATRICIAN

Before you begin your search for a pediatrician, find out specifics as to what type of expenses are covered by your insurance company. You might be surprised to find that your policy does not reimburse for "well visits" (regular checkups). Do your homework in advance, especially if you are thinking about canceling one form of insurance and keeping another.

• • •

Find a reputable pediatrician who has a lot of experience with multiples and premature infants. You can find a pediatrician by getting the opinions of other doctors in your area (ask your obstetrician), or by getting a general consensus from other mothers in your multiples club. *NOTE: It's best to find a pediatrician by the 28–30th week of pregnancy if you are expecting twins, and by the 26–28th week if you are having triplets.*

• • •

Not only is reputation important, so is the distance you will need to travel to the pediatrician. Traveling too far to a doctor's office will be inconvenient, considering the number of times you will need to pay him or her a visit in the first few years. Keep this in mind when choosing a doctor for your children. *NOTE: The American Academy of Pediatrics recommends checkups a few days after delivery, and 1, 2, 4, 6, 9, 12, 15 and 24 months of age.*

• • •

If the pediatrician has office hours on the weekends, if practical, try to schedule checkups during this time. Weekends are good for a number of reasons: 1) The office is generally not as crowded and chaotic; 2) There aren't as many sick children spreading germs; 3) The doctor usually has more time for you; and 4) Your spouse may be available to lend a hand.

• • •

Whenever you schedule an appointment, ask for the first appointment of the day — before the germs arrive!

• • •

If you bring more than one baby for an appointment, bring someone along to help you. Having an extra pair of hands is essential. Visits to the pediatrician can be a lot more work than you might think.

• • •

Find a neighbor or nearby friend you can count on for those situations when you have one sick child to bring to the pediatrician. I would like to say that these situations are few and far between, but sometimes this can happen on a weekly basis! Don't wait until a child gets sick to find someone. Line someone up as soon as possible.

• • •

There will be days when you will have no choice but to visit the pediatrician with no help. When this happens, ask one of the nurses for a few minutes of her time if you get desperate. Also note that when your children cry it will upset you more than anyone else.

• • •

Bring the following items when visiting the pediatrician with your infants:

1) 1 extra diaper per child
2) Wipes
3) 1 change of clothing

4) 1 bottle per child
5) 1 toy for each child
6) Daily schedule chart for the past week (or more)
7) A list of questions
8) Insurance card
9) Checkbook (or credit card)
10) Stroller
11) An extra pair of hands

• • •

Plan to arrive five to ten minutes early to your appointments to allow time for unpacking, unstrapping, undressing, and most importantly, unwinding! If you are rushed from the very beginning, this can be stressful and sometimes even disastrous!

• • •

Ask that your babies be checked in the order of their birth. The reality is, details about each child can become confused. Having an organized approach will help you, as well as the doctor, remember specifics about each child.

• • •

Whenever possible, avoid lugging your babies into the pediatrician's office in their infant car seats. If you use your stroller, it is much easier on your back, and it makes the logistics of getting your babies in and out of the office more manageable. Even a triple stroller works well.

• • •

Save yourself trips to the pharmacy by asking the office staff to call in prescriptions. When you do this, ask for samples to get you through the day and pick up the prescription at a more convenient time. If possible, take advantage of a drive-through pharmacy.

• • •

Keep your own immunization records for each child. When you keep a record keep track of: 1) Who was immunized; 2) What vaccinations were given; and 3) What was the exact date of the vaccination? Put your records in a place for safekeeping: You will refer to them when your children enter daycare or preschool. It is very common for dates to be missing, shots to be confused, or the data to be illegible when a doctor's office provides the information. Your records will clarify information and save you time when you need answers.

• • •

Ask the pediatrician for a schedule that lists all the required immunizations and the age at which they should be given. The schedule will assure you that your children are getting all of their shots on a timely basis, and it will serve as a reminder of when you will need to schedule an appointment.

RELATION-SHIPS
THAT PASS IN THE NIGHT

When I was expecting, I learned that the divorce rate among parents with multiple birth children is more than twice the average divorce rate. At the time I couldn't understand why, but now that I have been married for almost nine years and a mother of multiples for close to six, the statistic makes more sense. Don't let this alarm you, but your relationship will require a lot more work than it once did. No matter how important your relationship is to you, out of necessity, it will end up taking a back seat to the relationship you will have with your children.

...

When multiples arrive, relationships suffer as parents spend their days and nights caring for their children. Priorities change as parents find themselves running to a screaming child instead of spending time with their spouse. Even at night, parents often spend the last bit of energy they have preparing for the next day.

•••

Out of convenience or necessity, parents of young multiples find they don't do things as a family as often as they would like to. As an example, many find it easier for one parent to stay home with the kids while another runs errands, or one parent takes one child and runs in one direction while the other takes another child (or two) and runs in a different direction. Doing things as a family will require time and patience; things you won't have much of while your children are babies.

•••

Marriages are also strained when parents disagree on how to raise children, or when a husband or wife feels ineffective as a parent. According to *Parenting Magazine*, many times parents (particularly fathers) may not be as prepared for the lifestyle adjustments a new baby brings. With multiples, parents are sometimes blindsided by the new challenges involved, and this can lead to discomfort at home, including a relationship with a spouse.

•••

One of the most important things you can do for your relationship is to talk as much as you can before you become new parents. Both of you will have to be on the "same page" with regard to your expectations of the birth, otherwise arguments will erupt, adding even more stress to your relationship. Work through every detail you can think of (expectations of yourselves as well as each other) and come to an understanding before your children are born.

•••

In order for your relationship to thrive in the multiples mix, both you and your spouse will need to go out of your way to focus on your relationship. You will need to set aside time, as well as muster up the energy, at the end of the day to talk without interruption. If you want to enjoy each other's company on a regular basis, finding a reliable babysitter will be a must.

•••

Realize that the little things you do for each other can have a positive impact on your relationship and the attitude you have throughout the day. These don't require much energy but will be the glue that holds your relationship together. A simple compliment is sufficient, or even taking a minute to empty a dishwasher can do the trick!

• • •

Make every attempt to overindulge each other on special occasions. Because most days will be not so out of the ordinary, you should both make a point to make special days extra special.

• • •

When you are lucky enough to go out on a dinner date, forget about your responsibilities and try to avoid making your children the subject of every conversation. Dinner dates should be a special time set aside for the two of you, not your family. View this time as rare opportunity for couple time. *NOTE: According to the results of a survey conducted by MOST, 65% of parents with multiples get to go out as a couple less than six times a year.*

• • •

Be sensitive to each other's "space" and time with friends. If you go out one night and leave your children with your husband, expect to reciprocate. If there isn't a balance, someone is bound to feel resentful. Continuing to spend some time with friends will be a very important part of maintaining a happy relationship, no matter how busy you are.

• • •

Since traditional families typically do not include twins or triplets, don't expect a traditional family arrangement to work well for you (where the father works outside of the home and the mother cares for the house and children). It will be essential that both you and your spouse share in caring for your babies and with the chores around the house. Parents of multiples essentially have two jobs: one day job, and one that they need to share, at night.

• • •

When sharing the duties, do your best not to keep score: "Mom changed the last 237 diapers, Dad woke up early the last 8 mornings in a row and made dinner 4 times last week, Mom did 12 loads of laundry in two days." Doing this will only cause more tension!

• • •

Although you may think your relationship won't change, it will. During a group meeting on relationships, an expectant mother of triplets asked other mothers, "I don't understand. If you can all find time to shower every day, why can't you find some quality time for your spouse? I won't let that happen to me. My relationship is too important." Long story short, after she had given birth, I met her for dinner one night and she told me, "Everyone was right! Not only has my relationship changed, there are days when I don't even take a shower!"

•••

If you feel the need to rant and rave, or just need support from other mothers, visit the "Married with Twins" message board *(www.twins magazine.com)*. Sometimes it's very comforting to know you're not alone!

•••

Have no fear! Most relationships improve as multiples grow older and gain independence. Parents find time to take showers, aren't so exhausted, and manage to find more time for each other.

"My husband went from the top to the bottom of the food chain when we became parents."
— A quote from a mother in a *Time Magazine* article on relationships.

PARENTING PETS

Taking care of goldfish can prove to be difficult while caring for multiples! Your children will require every bit of energy you have. Spend it on them, not a neglected pet. Keep pets in mind when your children are old enough to take care of them and give them the love and attention they need.

•••

If your kitchen has a nice view of the outdoors, put a birdfeeder outside, a few feet from your kitchen window. When you do this, you'll be amazed at the enjoyment your children will get out of watching wild birds come to the feeder as you prepare meals. Outdoor birds are an excellent alternative to dogs or other pets that require lots of attention, particularly when your children are very young.

•••

Many parents of multiples say, "If I only had a dog to clean the kitchen floor of all the food!" Keep in mind that dogs will clean your floor, but many do not like bananas and other gooey things which are the most difficult to remove from floors. Use your mop instead.

•••

If you already have a dog, realize that some, particularly younger dogs, may confuse your babies with chew toys when they come home. It is their nature to want to play and to be very excited. Be careful to work out a plan for their introduction. At a minimum, make sure your dog has had adequate obedience training.

•••

Many families who already own pets often find they have the perfect family once their babies arrive. If a pet is already part of your family, you probably will find the extra work involved well worth your time.

MULTIPLE MEDICATIONS

Create your own medicine chart that you can reproduce for your refrigerator. There will be times when your children will be on various medications at the same time, and it can become confusing if you don't have a chart. This will also help you to remember to administer the drug(s). Here is a sample of what one might look like:

		BABY A				BABY B				BABY C			
MEDICATION	DATE	Amoxicillin			Fluoride	N/A			Fluoride	N/A			Fluoride
DAY		AM	12	PM	1× DAILY				1× DAILY				1× DAILY
Sunday	15-Jan					XX	XX	XX		XX	XX	XX	
Monday	16-Jan					XX	XX	XX		XX	XX	XX	
Tuesday	17-Jan					XX	XX	XX		XX	XX	XX	
Wednesday	18-Jan					XX	XX	XX		XX	XX	XX	
Thursday	19-Jan					XX	XX	XX		XX	XX	XX	
Friday	20-Jan					XX	XX	XX		XX	XX	XX	
Saturday	21-Jan					XX	XX	XX		XX	XX	XX	

•••

Be careful of dosage strengths! Surprisingly, most infant pain medications are concentrated and are actually stronger than children's medications. Whenever you administer any medication to your children, always use as directed, and be sure to use the dropper that comes with the medication to avoid further confusion.

•••

Administering double or triple doses of medication can be quite an undertaking! If a child refuses an over-the-counter medicine, put it in a bottle and mix it with a very small amount of formula, breastmilk, or juice. Do not do this with prescription medications because it is important that they ingest the entire amount, which sometimes doesn't happen when you try to trick them. *NOTE: If you really have a tough time offering medication, look for baby medicine dispensers or ask your pharmacist to flavor the medication.*

•••

Another trick is to pour the medication into a bottle nipple. As you hold the nipple pointing toward the floor, attach an empty bottle to it. Keep the bottle upside down and give it to your baby as if you were offering a bottle.

"Lay them flat on their backs and hold their hands over their heads (close to their head so they can't move it). Get them in position and use a dispenser to put the medication in the back of their mouths (toward the cheek so they do not gag). When I tried this, I could not believe how easy it was. It's a good idea to ask for help while doing this. You will also have to do this one child at a time!"
— Karen Z. (Mother of two young children)

SIMPLE THINGS THAT SIMPLIFY

Create or buy a "daily chart" to keep track of what your babies do throughout the day for the first few months. You will need this for your own information, for caregivers, and possibly for the pediatrician. You will use one chart per day, so make sure you have lots of copies. Here is a sample of what one might look like:

SAMPLE DAILY CHART

DATE: | Monday | | 1/15 |

BABY A					BABY B				
TIME	*BOTTLE	DIAPER	MEDS	OTHER	TIME	*BOTTLE	DIAPER	MEDS	OTHER
6:30 AM	4 oz	wet	eye drops		6:30 AM	3 oz	wet/bm		
10:00 AM	3 oz	wet/bm		very fussy	10:00 AM	4 oz	wet		
12:50 PM	3 oz	wet		nap 1.5 hrs	12:50 PM	3.5 oz	wet		nap 1 hr
4:15 PM	2.5 oz	wet			4:15 PM	3 oz	wet		
6:20 PM	3 oz	wet/bm	eye drops	nap 45 min	6:20 PM	3 oz	wet		nap 30 min
9:00 PM	4 oz	wet			9:00 PM	4 oz	wet		
11:15 PM	2 oz	wet		sleep	11:15 PM	4 oz	wet		sleep
2:45 AM	4 oz	wet			2:45 AM	3.5 oz	wet		
4:30 AM	3 oz	wet		awake!	4:30 AM	3 oz	wet/bm		good night

Replace "bottle" and "oz" with "time at breast" if you are breastfeeding.

• • •

You can create this chart on your computer. When you print it, make enough copies for a month to save yourself time. You may also want to spiral bind it to keep old, current and new charts at your fingertips.

• • •

Take a few minutes every week to take diapers out of their packages and stock them on a shelf or in a drawer. Keep them on each level of your home. This is guaranteed to save you time, especially when you need one *quickly*.

• • •

If you find that your multiples are in different diaper sizes, stock them in separate stacks on different shelves and draw a line with a permanent marker down the front the larger diapers ("L"ine = "L"arger). You can also tape the sizes on the base of the shelf and stack the correlating size on top of the label. Once you take diapers out of their package, it can be difficult to determine sizes because they are not individually labeled.

• • •

With twenty or thirty small nails to clip, simplify your weekly efforts by clipping nails while your babies sleep. Good luck otherwise!

• • •

It seems a mother's calendar is always full of contractor's visits, waiting for deliveries, the cable guy, and the like. Don't let these appointments continually wake your children from their naps or force you to stay home all the time. Schedule one day a month to deal with everyone whenever possible. Schedule all appointments on the same day, and enjoy all the other days in the month. *NOTE: If you have big household projects, take care of them prior to giving birth.*

• • •

If you plan to meet someone and bring your children, suggest an arrival time that allows for tardiness. For example, if you tell a friend you will meet her for a play date between 9:45 and 10:00 o'clock, it will take the pressure off of you to get there at a particular time. When you have yourself and small children to pack up, timing an arrival down to the minute can be difficult and stressful.

...

It's common to hear expectant mothers say, "There will be no television in this house!" I know an expectant mother of twins who was so adamant, she refused my offer of Sesame Street videos, and then lectured me about how bad television was for our children. Long story short: She had her babies, and the last time I went for a visit, she popped in a video as soon as I walked through her door! The lesson to be learned here is that "no television" is probably not a practical reality with multiples. Don't use your television as a babysitter, but consider it for those occasions when you really need a break (like time to brush your teeth!).

...

One of your daily grinds will be finding and putting on shoes. Not only will finding a match be a challenge, putting them on little feet will prove to be even more difficult. If someone gives you a hard time with shoes and you need to get somewhere, strap the child into a car seat and put the shoes on in the car. This makes the contest easier.

...

If you purchase two or three of something that requires assembly, do yourself a favor and pay an assembly charge if the store offers one. With multiples, "requires assembly" usually means "requires lots of time and patience."

"If you are expecting identical twins, make it easier on everyone to figure out who is who by putting a braided bracelet on one twins' wrist. This is more permanent and practical than polishing a big toe, especially in the winter months when toes are covered by socks. All you need to do it buy three strings of needlepoint thread and braid them into a bracelet."
— Margaret F. (Mother of 1-year-old identical twin boys)

VOLUNTEERED HELP

I am amazed at how many mothers of multiples tell me they didn't have help because they couldn't afford it. Realize that your help does not have to come in the form of paid help. Churches or other houses of worship are excellent places to inquire about volunteered help. You need not be a member to ask.

• • •

Put an ad in a local paper for a "short-term volunteer needed." There are plenty of people who would like to help others, especially if they know it's not a long-term commitment. *NOTE: Be sure to screen volunteers just as you would a paid employee.*

• • •

Contact your local Mothers of Multiples organization. Many offer meals for mothers and other support and assistance for those who ask for it.

• • •

When you find people to help you, be sure to scatter their arrival times. For example, if both sets of grandparents want to visit, ask one set to arrive first. Once they leave, arrange for the other set to visit. The same should go for anyone else who wants to volunteer his or her time. Try to solicit help, but be careful not to crowd your house! Having too much help can easily become more stressful than helpful. Take time to schedule volunteers, and be sure to explain the circumstances to family members to avoid hurt feelings.

• • •

Many expectant parents make the mistake of putting off visits from family members because they think it will be nice to have some "family time" together when the babies come home. If you are thinking you won't want company right away, trust me, you will! If anyone is kind enough to offer assistance, it will be in your best interest to accept it. *NOTE: It takes six to eight weeks to fully recover from a cesarean section! This also means no driving or climbing stairs.*

• • •

If friends or family members once offered to help you, you must assume they meant what they said. After the babies arrive, people sometimes feel as if they are intruding unless you solicit their help. If they offered to help, ask them to help.

• • •

Don't "expect" family members to help you. Many mothers have told me they couldn't believe that certain members of their own family never offered to help. Rather than creating a family squabble or cause yourself undue stress, try to accept the fact that your multiples are your responsibility, and not theirs. There is a real possibility that someone you thought would jump at the chance to help might not.

• • •

Neighborhood mother's helpers (9–12 years of age) can be a tremendous help. There is something about a young girl or boy and the special way they entertain babies and toddlers like no adult can. You will find your babies to be thoroughly entertained by them, and you will also find that you can get a fair amount of work done around your house while they find ways to amuse your children. *NOTE: Whenever a mother's helper is in your home, always keep in mind that he or she is a child in need of supervision as well.*

•••

Discuss small wages with a mother's helper's parent before offering any compensation. It could create an awkward situation if not discussed up front. Children 9–12 years of age are not usually looking for money, but rather a chance to play with your children. If they are older than 12 years of age, they are probably looking for a small wage, and rightfully so. At this age, they graduate from mother's helpers to babysitters.

•••

Ask a friend or relative to take one child for a day, night, or weekend. This is a win/win situation for everyone. You will be surprised at how this simplifies things, even if only for a short while.

•••

Create your own volunteers! When friends or relatives ask if they can come over for a visit, respond with, "Sure you can visit! Can I hand you a bottle when you get here?" Or, "Great! Would you mind if I took a 15-minute nap when you get here? Then we can have some coffee." They'll be happy to help out when you give them no choice, congenially, or course!

•••

Realize that volunteers do not necessarily have to care for your children. You can ask them to run errands, grocery shop, cook a meal, clean, do laundry, wash dishes, prepare bottles, and many other tasks.

•••

Be flexible with volunteered help and don't expect that volunteers will be with you everyday, or even every week. Try to find as many volunteers as you can, and schedule them whenever they are available.

•••

Don't forget to take advantage of your "free" babysitter — your husband. Let him take over whenever he can.

•••

If you are downright exhausted and desperate, be humble. Pick up the phone, explain your situation and ask for help. A true friend will always find a way to assist you.

•••

Never let a day go by without thanking those who volunteer to help you! You will want them to come back, won't you?

HIRING AND FIRING PAID HELP

I f you are on a budget and managed to set aside savings for a family vacation, opt to stay home and take the "vacation" in your house once your infants come home. Because you probably won't be going anywhere anytime soon, consider spending the money on hired help. Taking a "vacation" in your home will be the difference between enjoying and surviving the first few months with your newborns.

• • •

If you plan to hire help, hire after friends and family leave. The last thing you will want to do is pay someone to help while your house is busting at the seams with family and friends who are offering help at no cost. Of course if this will not be the case, plan to hire help sooner.

• • •

Although you should not hire help too soon, don't wait to find the right person to care for your children. The interview process could take quite some time. Start interviewing before you give birth and schedule an open-ended start date. Don't make the mistake of hiring help once you are at your wits end with exhaustion — plan ahead!

•••

When hiring, be very specific as to what the daily responsibilities will be. After the ground rules are established, they will be difficult to change. Have a checklist so nothing is forgotten and so you don't have to spend your energy reminding your help of his or her duties. I added a daily "to do" list to the bottom of a daily chart I created to keep track of feedings and other information about my triplets. By doing this, the list could not be ignored. The following is a sample of the list I used for hired help. Use it, and modify it to suit your needs:

Main Responsibilities:

- caring for, entertaining and playing with the children
- dressing
- diapering
- feeding/preparing meals
- bathing (when necessary)

"To Do" List:

- sweep/clean kitchen floor after meals
- clear and wash children's dishes
- empty dishwasher
- wash/sterilize bottles
- prepare bottles and stock refrigerator
- change crib sheets
- children's laundry (wash, dry and put back in drawers/closets)
- stock diapering station(s)
- clean crockpot (used for warming bottles)
- empty diaper pail(s)/take out garbage
- other _____

NOTE: These were the job requirements for a person I hired to care for my children in my home from 8 a.m. to 6 p.m. (while I worked). If you hire someone for fewer hours, don't expect that he or she will be able to accomplish everything on your list on a daily basis (most of these tasks were accomplished during naps times).

• • •

Unless you need someone during the day, consider help for the night-time before thinking about help during the daytime for the first few months. Nighttime *is by far* the most difficult. Many new mothers of multiples have told me that as long as they could get some sleep at night, they could handle anything during the day.

• • •

If you need help for a few months to get you through the feeding around the clock stage (perhaps for one or two nights a week to give you a break), think about contacting a professional caregivers' organization in your area by looking up "caregivers" in your phonebook. Many of their staff are well-trained caretakers, some of whom are nursing students who choose to work at night to put themselves through school. If you need imme-diate, short-term care you can rely on, this is a great solution.

• • •

Similarly, "postpartum doulas" specialize in helping families after the babies are born. They don't have medical degrees but are trained and experienced in providing care after childbirth. They do all sorts of things — caring for babies, breastfeeding advice, cooking and even light housework! Look to Doulas of North America (DONA International) *(www.dona.org)* for a postpartum doula locator by state.

• • •

If you can afford it, consider hiring a neonatal or baby nurse. Many parents hire these nurses from the hospital they delivered their babies in. Baby nurses are wonderful because you can hire them on a short-term basis, put trust in their abilities, and best of all, you can learn from their experience.

• • •

If you have babies who come home with oxygen, need medication or have medical issues, be sure to inquire about a professional nurse to help you at home while your babies are in need of extra care. These services are often covered by insurance. Keep in mind that you will have to ask for the assistance from your insurance company. Don't expect them to offer it if you don't inquire about it.

• • •

Before hiring a live-in nanny, contemplate "live-out" first, before asking someone to share your house, your food, possibly your car, and your personal space. Having an extra person living in your house can be very difficult, especially when you have a house full to begin with.

• • •

Are you serious about hiring live-in help? If so, think about this: Most live-in nannies do not go home on weekends. If you hire one, you may find yourself overwhelmed with your new responsibilities, and at the same time, feel "guilty" because your nanny has nowhere to go at night and on weekends. Although nannies are hired to help, they often take extra energy as you struggle to be cordial and find ways to make the nanny feel at home. *NOTE: Look to* www.gonannies.com, www.nannies 4hire.com *and* www.4nanny.com *for a nanny in your area.*

• • •

If you are thinking about hiring an au pair, realize that if things don't work out, it could be difficult to say "au revoir" to your au pair. Saying goodbye to an au pair is much more involved than saying goodbye to a local person you have hired. Certainly, there are many families who think au pairs are the greatest thing since sliced baguettes, and you may very well find that you are one of them. Just be sure to weigh your options before deciding to hire one. *NOTE: Look to* www.aupaircare.com *or* www.culturalcare.com *for more information.*

• • •

The newspaper is a popular way of finding help. Before you place an ad in the newspaper, look in the classified section under "situation wanted" or "childcare services." There are many people who advertise their childcare services, some of whom are individuals looking for jobs in the area. If you choose to advertise, look to a local newspaper and advertise there first: You may find many qualified candidates nearby.

• • •

If you are in need of part-time help, post signs at a local high school or college, or call and ask if they offer any childcare or early childhood education classes. If they do, ask for a name and number of the person who teaches the class. When you get in touch with the teacher, ask if he or she would announce your employment opportunity to the students.

•••

Always check references, even if you hire from an agency or hire someone based on a friend's recommendation. When talking to a reference, ask them to offer one "negative" about the person, even if they feel there really aren't any. Something that someone thinks is a slight negative about someone could be a significant negative to you. When you check references, find a pattern of consistency before concluding your phone calls.

•••

Not only should you check references, a Work & Family article I read in *The Wall Street Journal*, suggests that you should do a thorough background check before hiring a nanny. The article suggested using *www.USSearch.com* if you plan to use an online service as it is the most heavily used and their reports are very organized and accurate. You can also access online criminal records at *www.searchsystems.net* free of charge. If you think you can avoid a background check because you plan to hire from a nanny agency, think again. Only 50% to 75% of nanny agencies conduct background checks on applicants, based on surveys conducted by the *The Wall Street Journal*.

•••

Spend at least an entire day with a potential hire before you agree to employ the applicant. You will be amazed at what you might learn by the end of the day. I chose not to hire two people after spending a day with them. They both made excellent first impressions, and one even came recommended by a friend. Spend quality time with a potential hire before you run off to work and leave your kids in what you assume to be "capable" hands!

•••

If you plan to work and need to rely on someone, suggest that you both sign an informal "nanny agreement." This is not a formal document for which you need an attorney, but something you put together and jointly agree upon. Include the job requirements, caregiver's name, address, social security number (for tax purposes), hire date, hourly pay rate, work hours, vacation and other benefits. Along with this, ask for a two-week notice if the nanny decides to leave. Offer that you will do the same if things do not work out as planned. There is nothing you can do to stop someone from quitting and leaving on the same day, but with a signed agreement, there is some hope that you will not be left high and dry without a chance to find a replacement.

• • •

Consider hiring two babysitters on those occasions when you feel as if you might really need two. Some parents resort to this if they need to be away for an entire day or days, especially when their children are very young and require more care and attention.

• • •

Designate one parent to be in charge of hired help. He or she should be responsible for scheduling, payments, responsibilities, discussing issues about the children, and so on. If both parents are the "boss," it often results in confusion and aggravation for everyone, including your help. Having one person in charge is much better than two in this case.

• • •

If you hire someone and you find yourself doing more than 50% of the work or if you need to continually remind your hired help of her duties, find new help! There are some excellent nannies out there. Make sure you find a Mary Poppins and not a mediocre one. If you don't wake up every morning and think, "What would I do without my nanny?" but rather, "What should I do about my nanny?," it might be time to send her packing.

• • •

If you get a sense that your children are not comfortable or happy with their caretaker, you might want to consider new help. Before you make any decisions, make sure you have given your children adequate time to get to know their caretaker. A good indication of a problem might be if you sense that they are not happy when she arrives, and when you arrive back home, the mood hasn't changed for the better. If you are not certain, but simply "sense" that something is not right, it probably isn't.

• • •

Rates for babysitters and nannies vary considerably. The hourly rate depends on where you live, age and experience, and the number of children being cared for. Ask others in your area how much they pay and be sure you are dealing with comparable situations. Once you determine the going rate, start out with a slightly lower rate and suggest that you plan to offer an increase in pay after a few months, assuming all goes well. This will be an incentive for your hired help to work hard and for you to save some money.

· · ·

If you hire someone to provide care in your home and you pay the person more than $1,500 (threshold in 2007) throughout the year, be prepared to have hired a "household employee" according to the Internal Revenue Service. This will involve record keeping on your part: At a minimum, you will need to withhold Social Security and Medicare taxes from the employee (or pay them on the employee's behalf). You will also be required to report wages and possibly withhold and remit federal income and unemployment taxes during the year. Visit *www.irs.gov* for more information. When you get to the site, do a search on "household employees." *NOTE: You can avoid this if a caretaker provides services outside of your home (then you need to file a simple 1099MISC form).*

· · ·

Realize that some days you will rather have no help than have to hold a conversation with a person who is helping you. Having simple conversations can be exhausting. Don't get into the habit of socializing with help, especially when you are tired or have other chores to attend to. It's nice to be friendly, but your help must realize that you are a busy person and that they are there to help, not socialize.

· · ·

Don't be too flexible with paid help. If you are, you will regret it!

A BRIEFING ABOUT BREASTFEEDING

Breast milk is the best food a mother can offer her newborn babies. Breastfeeding for only a few weeks provides health benefits, and on a longer-term basis, gives babies the very best nutritional start in life. However, if you find that breastfeeding is not for you, don't feel guilty about your decision: You are not alone. According to the American Academy of Pediatrics, most mothers try to breastfeed, but only 30% of them make it to six months — and these are mothers of singletons!

...

If you breastfeed, expect to save some money. There are some expenses associated with breastfeeding, but the general difference in savings between breast and bottle feeding is the money you will save on formula. You can save about $600 if you breastfeed twins exclusively for the first three months. If you breastfeed triplets, the savings is about $900!

•••

Whether you plan to breast or bottle-feed your babies, the reality is that it's a lot of hard work! Plan on simultaneous feedings, whichever route you choose, as this will cut down on your stress level and the amount of fatigue accompanying your post-partum weeks and months. According to La Leche League International *(www.lalecheleague.org)*, women who breastfeed their twins save about 300 hours of effort a year! If you breastfeed, you won't have to prepare bottles (about 1,800 bottles *per child* in the first year), shop for formula, or sterilize anything.

•••

As mentioned previously (see section on THINGS TO CONSIDER/THINGS TO AVOID for details), you might find the following to be convenient for breastfeeding:

- Determination, education, and lots of patience
- Twin feeding pillow — "EZ-2-Nurse Twins" by Double Blessings
- Hospital-grade double breast pump (Medela or Ameda)
- Disposable breast pads and nipple cream
- Nursing bras/shawl/gowns/t-shirts
- Collection bags/bottles/nipples
- Vitamins, water, healthy snacks
- An extra breast and more time to sleep!

•••

Prepare in advance by gathering as much information as you can by visiting the following websites that are dedicated to breastfeeding multiples:

Articles/Frequently Asked Questions/General Information:

- *www.karengromada.com* — (Breastfeeding multiples specialist and author of Mothering Multiples)
- *www.lalecheleague.org/nb/nbmultiples.html* — (Answers to frequently asked questions, and articles)
- *www.twinstuff.com/breastfd1.htm* — (A series on breastfeeding twins)
- *www.parentingweb.com/lounge/multiples.htm#info* — (Breastfeeding more than one)

Breastfeeding Multiples — Mother-to-Mother Forums:

- *http://forums.llli.org/forumdisplay.php?f=40* — (La Leche League — breastfeeding premature infants)
- *http://forums.llli.org/forumdisplay.php?f=56* — (La Leche League — breastfeeding multiples)
- *www.twinsmagazine.com* — (Twins Magazine — go to "message boards," then "breastfeeding")
- *www.twinteresting.com/forums/breastfeeding/* — (Twinteresting — "Giving boob-tube and football-hold a whole new meaning")

Breastfeeding Triplets — Articles:

www.lalecheleague.org/NB/NBSepOct92p135.html
www.parentingweb.com/lounge/triplets.htm

• • •

Meet with a certified lactation consultant (CLC) who has experience assisting other mothers of multiples, and speak to her *before* you deliver. To find a lactation consultant in your area; call the maternity unit of the hospital where you plan to deliver, ask your obstetrician or pediatrician for a referral, or ask another breastfeeding mother of multiples. *NOTE: Most hospitals offer lactation consultation. If you deliver in a hospital with a level III NICU, there should be a consultant there to help you who has a great deal of experience working with new mothers of twins or more.*

• • •

If your babies are born prematurely and spend any time in an NICU, you will probably have no choice but to pump your breast milk for a few reasons: 1) Your babies may not be mature enough to breastfeed; 2) There is a chance they will have to be fed by a tube for a while; and/or 3) Nurses will have to feed your babies while you are away from the hospital. *NOTE: If you pump while your babies are in the NICU, talk to an on-staff lactation consultant about making a transition to the breast when your newborns are mature enough. This can be done while they are still being cared for in the hospital.*

• • •

Giving birth to premature babies is by no means a reason not to breastfeed! In fact, it should give you even more incentive. The American Academy of Pediatrics' Committee on Nutrition suggests that pumping your breast milk is the best thing you can do for your premature babies, because the milk of a mother who has given birth prematurely is different from a mother who carries her babies to term. "Pre-term breast milk" is actually higher in certain nutrients and more suitable for the needs of premature babies. Breast milk is also easier to digest and better tolerated by preemies.

• • •

For convenience while you pump, you can make your own hands-free breast pump bra. Simply cut two horizontal slits in the bottom of a snug sports bra (along the elastic in the bottom of the cup — the holes should be just large enough so that the suction cups will fit through them). Next, place the suction cups inside the holes, pull the bra up over your breasts and begin pumping. When you finish pumping, pull the bra down to its normal position.

With some knowledge and patience, it *is possible* to breastfeed two babies simultaneously! I have asked Sandy Clark, mother of twins, breastfeeding multiples expert, and inventor of the EZ-2-Nurse Twins Nursing Pillow to tell you about her product and discuss how this is done. If you plan to purchase this pillow, it will help to read and understand how to use it before you give birth. The following are Sandy's words of wisdom, product information, and step-by-step directions on how to use the pillow:

(A mother breastfeeding her newborn twins with the EZ-2-Nurse Twins (foam) Nursing Pillow)

(A mother using the EZ-2-Nurse (inflatable) Nursing Pillow)

Pillow features:

The EZ-2-Nurse Twins Nursing (foam) Pillow by Double Blessings is made of durable, precision-cut foam. It comes with a machine washable zippered cover and an additional "lower back" pillow for added support. The pillow supports up to 70 pounds, and secures behind mother with a buckle and adjustable strap that will fit up to a 54" waist.

Special design:

When we first designed this pillow, we wanted to emulate the position of how a mother brings a baby to her breast in the bend of her arm. Notice how the babies (in the photos) are coming to their mother at an angle. Our "angled" top surface allows you to bring your babies to the pillow, and position them on their sides, so that they face you to nurse. When babies nurse tummy-to-tummy (their tummy to your tummy), it's more natural, more comfortable, and more productive (for all of you). *NOTE: A baby should never be placed on a flat surface to nurse, because then he'll have to turn his head sideways to meet the breast. Not only is this position uncomfortable, it also impedes the natural swallow reflex and digestion.*

Hands-free breastfeeding:

Women ask me, "Will I *really* be able to nurse my twins *hands-free?*" Absolutely! Most nursing pillows show a mother cradle-holding one baby on top of a pillow, using the pillow for her arm support. This works great when nursing just one baby, but as a mother of multiples, you'll need to have both arms free so that you can bring your babies to the pillow surface one at a time, and then, when the nursing session is finished, be able to remove them from the pillow one at a time. Without a double, angled-cut top surface, you will not be able to do this safely or effectively.

With both hands free, you will have all ten fingers to assist with:

- latch-on and latch-off (place your forefinger between his gums to release his latch)
- chin-drop (if baby's bite is too small on your nipple, use your thumb and forefinger to drop his chin, which opens his mouth wider for a bigger latch)
- cheek-strokes (stimulate a sleepy baby by rubbing his cheek with the side of your forefinger)
- caressing (their silky little heads)
- burping one baby while the other one continues to nurse
- tending to a third or fourth child (you really *are* an amazing woman!)

Where to nurse:

The best place to nurse is on a sofa, loveseat, on top of your bed, or sitting straight-legged on the floor (as long as you have a wall or sofa to scoot up against for back support). *NOTE: Rockers or recliners don't work well because there isn't enough width between the arms of the chair for the pillow to fit properly. More importantly, you will need a place with a flat working surface on either side of you to safely place the babies prior to bringing them to the pillow.*

Positioning/Getting ready to nurse:

Before you sit down, place the babies within arm's reach *of where you will be sitting,* with one baby on the right, and one on the left. With the angled side up, strap the U-shaped pillow around you. *NOTE: It's easier to put the pillow on "backwards" with the buckle in front of you. Note the "click" as you connect the buckle, cinch the belt so the pillow is snug around you, then "spin" the pillow around, so the nursing surface is now in front of you.*

Once the pillow is in place, sit down between your babies, and place the back pillow (rounded end facing up) behind your lower back, so you can comfortably lean forward into the pillow. Bring one baby to the top of one side of the pillow, roll baby toward you and assist with latch-on. Slowly reach for the second baby, and repeat.

Finally, take a big breath, exhale, relax, and begin nursing. Note that although you'll be using the "football-hold" position (one baby along each side of you), your arms and hands should not be underneath the babies. They should be above the babies, free to assist with positioning, stimulating and caressing.

Burping:
When one baby is finished nursing, roll him over onto his tummy (on top of the nursing pillow), and rub his back until you get a burp. When finished, safely remove him from the pillow to where he started. Now, burp the second baby the same way, but bring him to the center and rub his back. *NOTE: If you prefer, remove both babies from the pillow, and then burp them individually on your shoulder.*

Bottle feeding:
If you "flip" the pillow over, the bottom surface of the pillow is flat. This is more compatible for bottle-feeding. Anyone can wear the pillow…Dad, Grandma, nanny, or babysitter. Just like you would during the day for nursing, bottle feeders can bring the babies to the pillow for completely comfortable bottle-feeding sessions.

Questions/Where to buy:
The EZ-2-Nurse Twins feeding pillow is the best-selling double breast-feeding pillow on the market, and is highly recommended by other moms of multiples. The pillow can be purchased on Sandy's website, *www.doubleblessings.com* (foam $48/inflatable $40). If you have any questions, call to speak with Sandy Clark at (619) 741-8623.

Women have had success breastfeeding two or more in the following ways:

- Breastfed exclusively — two at a time.
- Got comfortable feeding one baby at a time, then began double feeding sessions.
- Breastfed exclusively — usually one at a time.
- Breastfed for a few weeks for the nutrients — then switched to bottle feeding.
- Supplemented their breast milk with formula — especially mothers with triplets.
- Breastfed one baby and propped a bottle to feed the other(s) — when their babies were ready for the next feeding, they rotated them.
- Pumped exclusively — finding that allowing others to help was the key to their success.

In a nutshell, there is no breastfeeding technique that is "best" or suitable for everyone. Find what works for you and try your best!

• • •

For further guidance, purchase a book that is dedicated to breastfeeding multiples: *Mothering Multiples: Breastfeeding and Caring for Twins or More* by Karen Kerkoff Gromada, or *Breastfeeding for One, Two, Three, A Nursing Mother's Survival Guide* by Maria McCarthy.

• • •

A few years ago, two members of La Leche League International *(www.lalecheleague.org)* were guest speakers at a mothers of multiples meeting I attended. The women were very knowledgeable about breast-feeding, but since neither one of them had experience breastfeeding multiples, they had little to offer other than to tell the women in the group how "simple" it was. Some tension built as the mothers who breastfed (or tried) suggested it was not easy, but rather, quite difficult with multiples. Don't feel obliged to listen to people who tell you how "simple" breastfeeding multiples can be if they haven't done it themselves, and on the flip side, don't let anyone tell you it can't be done! Deciding to breastfeed or not should be your decision and no one else's.

•••

Some might think the difficulty with breastfeeding multiples is how to master the technique of either double pumping or feeding two at a time. No doubt, there can be difficulty in doing this, but the true test will be whether you can overcome fatigue and successfully breastfeed and/or pump around the clock for weeks or months on end. Breastfeeding twins and especially triplets is a true test of one's commitment and endurance. There is nothing any book can offer or any conversation you can have with anyone that will fully prepare you. Only time will tell if you will have success with it for any length of time. If you do, it's an experience rivaled by no other!

"I was totally committed to breastfeeding my triplets until I found myself double pumping, triple feeding, dripping, leaking, fatigued, frustrated and fed up!"
— Words from a former breastfeeding advocate and mother of bottle-fed triplets

---

"Realize that breastfeeding is not an "all or nothing situation." This is what helped me when I made the decision to breastfeed my triplets. It's hard, but it can be done!"
— Jen C. (Mother of triplets who breastfed and pumped for more than two years)

NOT-SO-BASIC BOTTLE-FEEDING BASICS

If you choose to bottle feed your multiples, you will be making choices about what kind of bottles to use. If you are on a tight budget, consider a no frills standard baby bottle. If you think you might resort to propping a lot of bottles, consider an angled bottle. If you are concerned about sterilization, consider using disposable bottles. If you are serious about breastfeeding, consider Advent bottles. *NOTE: All but the standard bottle claim to reduce colic, so don't let this be a factor in your decision making process! ANOTHER NOTE: Make sure your babies don't have difficulty drinking from the bottles before taking all of them out of their packages. This is common, especially with Playtex bottles.*

...

If you need them, ask the hospital staff for a few extra preemie bottles (2-ounce bottles) before you leave. They are difficult to find elsewhere. Preemie bottles are handy for measuring intake, and provide parents with milliliter information, as opposed to ounces.

• • •

Consider color or character coding bottles to help determine who has eaten and who's bottle is who's. It's less confusing. Another option is to put first initials on the side of the bottle with a permanent marker.

• • •

Mothers who bottle feed their babies also have to deal with "nipple confusion" in a slightly different way than breastfeeding mothers. If you are confused about whether to use silicon or latex nipples, I will offer my two cents and recommend silicon. I used both and found that silicon is more durable. *NOTE: Some bottles don't allow a choice, so make a decision about bottles first and then make a decision about nipples, assuming you have a choice.*

• • •

Expect to bottle feed your newborns about eight times a day each, around the clock for several weeks, or several months depending on birth weight. The feedings will generally range from every 2½ to 4 hours, and the amount they consume at each feeding may vary considerably. *NOTE: If you do some quick math, this means you will prepare about 1,460 bottles for twins, and 2,190 bottles for triplets in the first three months!*

• • •

When a nurse sends you home from the hospital with your babies and tells you to "feed them every 3½ to 4 hours," you shouldn't take her literally. Each child will have very different and unpredictable eating patterns to start. They may be hungry more often than you'd expect (sometimes as often as every half hour), or less often, depending on the day and the child. The nurse's instructions should be considered a general rule of thumb. If a baby cries uncontrollably, the first thing to do is try to feed him, even if he just ate. More often than not, you will find the crying was due to hunger.

• • •

It usually takes 35–45 minutes to bottle feed *one* premature baby and slightly less time for a full-term newborn infant. If you plan to feed your twins (or triplets) one at a time, expect a good part of your days and nights to be spent feeding them. This is why propping bottles is so common with feeding multiples.

• • •

Since you will have numerous feedings each day, offer your babies nipples that are intended for older babies (such as "stage 2" or "6 months") as soon as you feel comfortable that they are sucking and drinking well. Nipples intended for older babies will reduce your feeding times because they allow for faster flow.

• • •

Newborn babies need to drink about 2.5 ounces of formula per pound of weight per day. In other words, a "typical" 5½-pound newborn twin should drink about 13.75 fluid ounces a day, or 1.75 ounces at each feeding (this is **one-fifth** of a standard 8 oz. bottle!) A "typical" 3¾-pound newborn triplet should drink about 9.4 ounces, or about 1.2 fluid ounces at each feeding (or **one-eighth** of a standard 8 oz. bottle!) — this is why preemie bottles can be very helpful for measuring intake. If you have any concerns or questions about feeding, especially if the amount your child(ren) are consuming is consistently less than 2.5 ounces per pound of weight, be sure to share this with your babies' pediatrician. *NOTE: To calculate the daily intake needed: (baby's weight × 2.5 = fluid ounces needed).*

• • •

Newborns feed more often but drink considerably less formula per feeding than older babies. As your babies get older and begin to sleep through the night, the number of bottles they consume per day will be reduced to about 5 or 6, although they will actually be drinking more formula.

• • •

When you prepare bottles, you may find it convenient to prepare several at once. Making enough bottles for a full day (8 bottles per child) works well. *NOTE: Some mothers prefer to prepare bottles on an "as needed" basis. This is common with those who use powdered formula and choose to store it in a pitcher. Try both methods and see what works best for you.*

• • •

If you plan to use powdered or liquid-concentrate formula, you will need a plastic two-quart "pouring" pitcher with a lid to mix the formula. The kind of pitcher doesn't matter, as long as it is at least two quarts in size and has a lid that closes. *NOTE: Those with triplets might want to consider two two-quart pitchers, or a gallon-sized one.*

• • •

Get into the habit of changing your newborns' diapers *before* you feed them. This should stimulate them enough so that they feed well. Newborns are known for falling asleep before they finish feeding, which can be frustrating for any parent who needs to feed more than one. Once they can get through feedings without falling asleep, you will probably find that it makes more sense to change them after they have eaten.

• • •

Another way to stimulate a baby so that he drinks more is to move the nipple in an up/down motion to let him know that the nipple is there. When you do this, move the nipple up and down in the mouth (roof of mouth then down to tongue) and not in and out.

• • •

Crockpots make heating multiple bottles a snap, and they tend to heat more evenly than microwave ovens (which are not recommended). Keep about two inches of water heated in it throughout the day, and put it on low.

• • •

When your babies are old enough to hold a bottle but not yet coordinated enough to lift it up to their mouths to drink in an upright position, sit them in their car seats in the lowest reclining position. They tend to have no problem feeding themselves in this position as soon as they can hold a bottle with two hands. This is huge milestone and is one of their first steps to independence!

• • •

Feeding gets more difficult when your babies begin to eat solid food. Bottle feeding is not nearly as messy, you can feed just about anywhere, and you always know what is on the dinner menu! Enjoy the simplicity while it lasts.

"I used a funnel when I poured formula into bottles.
It was less mess and reduced bottle preparation time."
— Ruth N. (Mother of GG twins)

FORMULA AND OTHER FLUIDS

Probably the easiest way to understand some of the more popular brand name baby formulas would be to compare them to the grades of gasoline! They offer three choices that vary in price and serve the same purpose. The least expensive choice would be "regular" (powder), the next choice, "plus" (liquid concentrate), and the most expensive would be "super" (ready-to-feed). Like gas, where you decide to purchase your formula will determine the price. If you shop around, you can save a few cents per quart.

• • •

The best place to buy powdered formula is in wholesale stores because they offer large containers of it, although they don't offer many choices. For liquid concentrate and ready-to-feed, there is no obvious best place to shop, although grocery stores tend to be a bit more expensive than stores such as Wal-Mart and Target.

• • •

If you feed two 10-pound babies, a day's worth of formula (50 fluid ounces of Enfamil) should cost you (grocery store prices):

Ready to feed: $7.13 (one month: $216.87)
Concentrate: $6.25 (one month: $190.10)
Powder: $5.19 (one month: $157.86)

• • •

If you feed three 10-pound babies, a day's worth of formula (75 fluid ounces of Enfamil) should cost you (grocery store prices):

Ready to feed: $10.69 (one month: $325.15)
Concentrate: $9.38 (one month: $285.31)
Powder: $7.78 (one month: $236.64)

• • •

The savings of powder over ready-to-feed is substantial: $59 savings per month (for twins); $89 savings per month (for triplets). Or an annual savings of $708 for twins and $1,068 for triplets.

• • •

Expect to pay the following for *one* full (8 oz) bottle of brand-name formula (grocery store prices):

Ready to feed: $1.14
Concentrate: $1.00
Powder: $.83

• • •

Although powdered formula is the least expensive form of formula on the market, you might want to consider ready-to-feed formula for the first month or so. Keep things as simple as possible until you have a chance to recuperate and get your "new mother" act together. *NOTE: Ready-to-feed will also be more convenient because your babies will start out by drinking very little per feeding. Small amounts of formula can be tough to mix and measure.*

• • •

I personally don't know many parents who have fed their multiples ready-to-feed formula for more than the first month or two, unless their babies had medical issues that forced them to use it. In most situations (but certainly not all), ready-to-feed formula is not an economical option for those with twins or more. Not only is it expensive, you will need a forklift to haul it out of the store!

• • •

If you use powdered formula, you can avoid clumping by preparing bottles about an hour in advance of when you would like to use them. It is best to mix the powder with warm water, and when you stir, use a whisk. After stirring, put the lid on and shake vigorously for about one minute. When you are finished shaking, let the formula stand in your refrigerator for about an hour, and then shake it vigorously once again before you use it.

• • •

If you don't like mixing powder but don't want to spend the money on ready-to-feed formula, buy concentrated liquid formula instead of powder. Mixing is easy and clumping is eliminated; all you do is add water.

• • •

Consider generic baby formula if money is a concern. The contents in every can of baby formula sold in the United States is regulated by the federal government, thanks to the Infant Formula Act passed by Congress in 1985. As a result of this act, generic formulas are reported to have very similar nutrients to their more expensive competitors. Their prices are also 25–35% less than the highly-marketed brands!

• • •

Aside from the typical choices offered by manufacturers, there are other formulas on the market for specific needs, including soy-based formulas, milk-based, hypoallergenic, low iron, with iron, pre-thickened, lactose-free, and so on. Talk to your pediatrician about what's best for your babies and don't make your own decision.

• • •

Before you start feeding your babies formula, realize that all brands will stain carpeting and clothing unless you remove it immediately!

• • •

Before you know it, you will blink and your formula days will be over. The transition to milk usually happens when your children are about 12 months of age. Before you offer milk, you will need to discuss when to make the transition, as well as what kind of milk to use, with your children's doctor.

• • •

When you buy milk you will no longer be able to stock up as you once did with formula. You will find yourself running to the store on average two or more times a week for fresh milk. Reduce your trips to the store by asking your spouse to be the "milk man" on his way home from work. Or, it might make sense to have milk delivered to your home. Believe it or not, the "milk man" still exists in many towns (there is a milk man in my town — and I live in New Jersey where there aren't many cows to speak of!). Look under "milk products — retail" in your local phone book. *NOTE: Another reason to hire a milkman: one gallon of milk weighs 8½ pounds!*

• • •

Save money by comparing juice labels. Many bottles (such as apple) have the same ingredients as those expensive "baby" juices. Be sure to check that the vitamins and contents are the same, and that you are buying 100% juice. If you take time to look, you will find the same juice in a different container for a much cheaper price.

• • •

When you offer juice, get into the habit of diluting it with water. It's cheaper, and reduces the amount of sugar. The best part is you are not shopping for juice as often.

• • •

Offer water as an alternative to juice. If you set the rules and stick to them, you will have your children drinking more water in no time.

ASSEMBLING YOUR ASSEMBLY LINE: FEEDING TECHNIQUES

When the time comes to feed your twins or triplets, you will quickly gain a better understanding of why humans were not meant to give birth to more than one child at a time! Because chances are good you will not get an extra appendage as a shower gift, you will need to make optimal use of the two arms you have by being creative with your feeding techniques.

...

Lesson #1 when feeding multiples: Don't expect to feed yourself and your babies at the same time. This will not happen for quite some time! Lesson #2: Always anticipate when your children will become hungry and have something prepared about 10–15 minutes beforehand. If you wait until the last minute, feedings will be more challenging.

· · ·

It's fine to prop bottles, but don't prop exclusively. Whenever practical, hold your babies when you feed them. If you prop bottles, remember to keep your children in sight at all times. Propped bottles can cause babies to choke, spit up, or have other problems during the feeding process.

· · ·

For bottle-feeding two at a time, use a "Back Jack" floor chair *(www.fourgates.com)* and position yourself comfortably on the floor. After you are seated, extend your legs out in front of you, then bend your right knee out to the right of you and your left knee out to the left of you (with the heels of your feet touching one another). Place one infant on his back, in the crook of one knee and another against the crook of your other knee. You can easily feed two babies this way as you comfortably hold a bottle in each one's mouth.

· · ·

For simultaneously bottle-feeding triplets, follow the same steps above and place a third baby in an infant car seat beside you. Recline the car seat to a 45-degree angle and prop a bottle. This is a very simple way to simultaneously feed three at a time. *NOTE: You can also use a boppy pillow or bouncy seat, although using a car seat is easier.*

· · ·

Another feeding technique: Use "Podee Hands-Free" baby bottles. Place the bottle between your babies' legs and extend the nipple portion up to their mouths. *NOTE: There are some negatives to using Podee bottles: 1) The tubing can be difficult to clean; 2) The nipple often falls out of babies' mouths; and 3) They use a "standard" bottle nipple which might be a difficult transition for babies who have not used one. You can buy Podee Hands-Free bottles at Babies "R" Us, or you can view a list of other retailers by visiting* www.podee.com. *ANOTHER NOTE: Pacifeeders are a comparable product and can be found online at* www.savi-baby.com.

· · ·

Another bottle propping device is "The Extra Hand — Flexible Baby Bottle Holder." This is a simple metal gadget that attaches to an infant car seat. All you need to do is place a bottle in the clip and position it toward the baby. I have used these as well as Podee bottles, and preferred the Extra Hand. You can find these for sale at *www.extrahandproducts2.com.* *NOTE: The Bottle Nanny is a comparable product and can be found online at* www.babydoodads.com.

For other bottle propping devices visit the following websites: *www.babacaddy.com, www.bottlesling.com, www.bottletenders.com, www.greatbabyproducts.com* (Milk Maid bottle holders), and *www.littlewonders.com*. All of the products mentioned work well for propping bottles.

• • •

If you prefer the traditional way of propping bottles, roll two receiving blankets together into a tube shape and place them on either side of the baby. When you have the blanket tube in position, rest a bottle on a 45-degree angle with the nipple pointing toward your baby's mouth.

• • •

Small stuffed animals are also very useful for propping bottles. Many of them are the perfect shape, size, and thickness for holding bottles in place.

• • •

Having twins or triplets does not mean that you need to be ultra-efficient by doing everything two or three at time. During the day, your goal should be not to feed your babies simultaneously, but to feed one right after another. Unless they are both/all crying for a bottle, enjoy one-on-one time with each child whenever possible. *NOTE: Feeding in the wee hours of the night is a different story! At night it makes sense to prop bottles, or do anything possible to feed your babies simultaneously. Spend as little time as you can feeding at night and as much time as you can sleeping.*

• • •

There are many bottle-feeding techniques. Ask other parents of multiples what has worked best for them and try their technique, or be creative and discover your own.

• • •

When the time comes, you will probably be offering solid foods before your babies will be able to sit in highchairs. To start, feed them in their car seats, adjusted to the most upright position. You can easily feed your multiples by lining them up (side-by-side) in their infant car seats on your kitchen floor. *NOTE: Some mothers use Boppy pillows for feeding at this stage. Others use BebePods (www.bebepod.com) or Bumbo Seats (www.bumboseat.com).*

• • •

When your babies are old enough to sit in high chairs or other seats (see THE LOW DOWN ON HIGHCHAIRS), use the same side-by-side feeding technique. By the time your babies are able to sit in highchairs, they will be much better eaters and the feedings will get easier. You will also be able to sit like a normal human being on a kitchen chair as you feed!

"Don't feed the same baby twice…this happened to me!" — Fred L. (My husband)

CONTINUOUS CRYING

Crying is your babies' first language. It is their only method of communicating while they are too young to speak. Rather than becoming frustrated by their cries, appreciate the fact that they are able to communicate at such a young age. Your challenge will be to understand them!

· · ·

Experts claim that newborn babies cry between 2½ and 3 hours a day. This doesn't seem like much at first glance. But realize that this equates to about 25% of their wake time during the day. If you add another sibling or two, your babies probably will spend more time crying than doing anything else during their wakeful periods. Does this make your hair stand on end? It should! Crying, especially in the early months, can bring the toughest of parents to tears!

• • •

Many parents claim that their biggest stress about parenting young multiples is their babies' continuous crying. For the first several months, expect crying to be a constant in your home. As a parent, no matter how hard you try, your babies' crying will be something that you will never get used to.

• • •

Babies cry because they are either:

- hungry
- tired
- have gas discomfort
- in an uncomfortable position
- too warm
- too cold
- need a diaper change
- need to suck
- want attention
- startled by something
- not feeling well

Review this list when your children cry in an attempt to understand and settle them.

• • •

FACT: Some babies need to "cry it out" before they can relax and fall asleep. In these situations, there will be nothing you can do to sooth your babies. Although difficult, accept this when it happens, and try not to waste too much energy on something you will have no control over.

• • •

To help comfort your babies, offer them something to cuddle such as a baby blanket or stuffed animal. Having a "security blanket" tends to calm them, especially when they are tired. *NOTE: Do not offer these to sleep with when they are infants!*

• • •

Put your most demanding baby in a sling, or just cuddle and carry him while you take a scenic tour of your house. Offer a breast, bottle or pacifier while you are doing this. Movement and sucking are known to be a good combination. Unfortunately, this may not be practical if you have more than one upset baby and no one to help you.

• • •

Consider packing up and going for a drive. This will require work on your part, but once you are on the road, the sound and motion of the car may help your babies to relax and perhaps fall asleep. Going for a drive is often an excellent remedy for crying.

• • •

If you have a child who is incessantly crying or is irritable, try giving him a warm bath. This can have a soothing effect because it relaxes muscles, and can distract him from whatever was bothering him. *NOTE: If your baby is screaming out of control don't do this!*

• • •

One desperate measure that usually works is to turn your hairdryer on low with no heat, and let some air blow on their faces; hold the hairdryer about one foot away from the baby's face. Doing this should stop them from crying, at least temporarily. For some reason, hairdryers are good distractions to incessant crying.

• • •

If possible, provide your baby with a calm, quiet atmosphere in a room with no television or other crying babies. Sometimes a room full of chaos and noise can wreak havoc on everyone.

• • •

If continuous crying is getting the best of you, use an iPod for a few minutes. While listening, start singing!

• • •

When you've had enough crying for one day, or maybe even a lifetime, hand your babies over to someone else for a break. Even the shortest breaks can do wonders for worn out parents. If you do this, you may be surprised to find that a different face might be just what they wanted!

• • •

When the going gets tough and you have no one to help you, give yourself a time out. Leave the room if you have to, and take some deep breaths as you regroup and calm your nerves. Before you leave the room, be sure that your children are contained and safe.

• • •

Parents sometimes find themselves disenchanted when their children reach a certain "magical" age only to find that crying persists. Expect that parenting will become less stressful, but crying will continue to be very much a part of your daily life for quite some time.

"A good friend of mine gave birth to triplets four months ago. I decided to give her a break and went to spend a weekend with her last month. I couldn't believe the chaos! Someone was crying the entire time I was there! I felt like popping one of her Zolofts by the end of the weekend. I couldn't handle it...and I'm a mother of two."
— Words from my kids' hairdresser.

"I take long walks to my mailbox when my twins won't stop crying."
— Beth Y. (Mother of 6-month-old GG twins and an older daughter)

COULD IT BE...COLIC?

Colic affects about 1 in 5 newborns. Given that you are expecting multiples, your chance of having a child with colic has increased significantly. Do your best to accept this possibility.

• • •

If a child has colic, he usually begins to show symptoms around two to three weeks of age. Colic should peak between six and eight weeks, and should be gone by four months of age. Colic will be predictable in that your child will cry at the same time every day, or nearly every day. Although there is no exact definition, colic is typically three hours of non-stop crying a day. If you have a colicky child, expect the crying to last for at least three weeks, at least three times a week.

• • •

Although no one knows for sure, poor digestion is thought to cause colic. There are lots of remedies but no real cure for colic. The best way to treat colic is to try different potential remedies, and if you find one that works, stick with it. Note that there is no remedy that works best, and keep in mind that there is a chance nothing will offer relief. All babies respond differently to various remedies.

• • •

If one of your babies has colic it will be obvious. Colic is different from a normal cry. Your colicky child will scream much longer and with greater intensity than his sibling(s). My son had colic, and when he cried, he screamed non-stop as if someone had put a dagger in his chest (this is the only way I can describe it in words). The cry sounded like a very painful, as opposed to irritable, cry. *NOTE: Making a distinction in cries between siblings will not be easy if they both/all have colic!*

• • •

If you suspect colic, schedule an appointment with your child's pediatrician. The pediatrician should do a thorough exam to rule out anything other than colic that might be causing the discomfort. When babies are colicky, there is usually relief throughout the day. If the crying is constant and lasts all day, be sure to have your baby checked without delay.

• • •

Keeping babies in an upright position after each feeding tends to reduce colic. It might help to sit (and strap) your babies into their infant car seats in an upright position to assist you in doing this.

• • •

You might be able to offer some relief by inquiring about a formula change. Your baby may have an allergy to the formula he is drinking, or the formula may simply not agree with him. If you change formulas, don't expect any improvement for at least five days. The colic may not improve at all, but it's worth a try.

• • •

Some parents resort to using Nutramigen baby formula for colic. This is often purchased after all other possible remedies have been exhausted: Nutramigen costs about 50% more than other ready-to-feed formulas. Nutramigen is marketed as "easy to digest" and is hypoallergenic. *NOTE: Alimentum (a similar product) also reduces symptoms of colic.*

• • •

Try the "colic hold" suggested by La Leche League International. Place your baby's stomach down along your arm with his head resting in the crease of your arm (at your elbow) with his legs straddling either side of your hand. Keep him in this position as you move about or rock him. Gently rub or pat his back in an attempt to further soothe your baby.

...

Some other mother-tested remedies for colic:

- Burp more often
- Use infant gas drops
- For severe colic, ask the pediatrician for medication
- Sing lullabies as you rock them, or try a swing
- Offer pacifiers
- Place a warm washcloth over their bellies
- Use downward stokes as you massage bellies with lotion
- Purchase Gripe Water (in pharmacies, or *www.great babyproducts.com*)
- Breastfeeding mothers should avoid eating foods that cause gas, such as milk products, broccoli, caffeine, and nuts

...

I have personally tried most of these suggestions only to conclude that "time" was the only thing that worked for my son. Nothing worked, not even the expensive formulas marketed for colicky babies. Try a few suggestions described above, and if they work, great! Otherwise, don't drive yourself crazy trying to find a remedy that may not exist.

...

One positive note on my personal experience with colic: Today my once colicky son is the most patient, well-behaved child I have. I am not sure if there is any correlation to his colicky start in life, but I do know that colic is temporary and is no indication of a particularly demanding personality. Keep this in mind when the going gets tough.

...

Some studies suggest that colicky babies are particularly intelligent and have superior social and cognitive skills as compared to babies who have never had colic. This might be the case because fussy babies tend to be held and comforted more. Although difficult, try to maintain a positive attitude as you realize the extra comfort and attention you offer may not cure colic, but could ultimately be the best medicine.

...

Keep in mind that colic is not an illness but a condition that your babies *will* outgrow.

FEELING BLUE

Having realistic expectations about what to expect after the birth of your multiples is the key to really enjoying them. If your expectations are "rose colored" or too high, you are going to be in for a big surprise. The reality is, there will be many days where you would "rather be in prison," as my husband once graciously put it. Your expectations should be realistic with regard to your babies, as well as about what to expect of yourself.

• • •

As the saying goes, "You are in charge of your own attitude." This is not always the case when you have multiples. When you are outnumbered everyday, often the children's attitude can become your own attitude. Some days seem endless, and others are a pure joy, primarily depending on the mood of those who outnumber you.

...

Not only can children influence your mood throughout the day, realize that you can influence their's as well. I found that "shifting gears" really helped me to get through some tough periods throughout the day. If your children happen to be particularly irritable and you are feeling grumpy yourself, don't expect the mood to change for quite some time. If you sense this in your children, and yourself, make every effort to switch gears and turn on a happy face. Before you know it, your happy face will influence others to put on their's as well!

...

Baby blues is very common and affects 50–75% of all new mothers. It usually occurs within a few days after delivery, and symptoms include crying for no reason, irritability, anxiety, impatience, or restlessness. Because you are expecting more than one baby, your chance of experiencing baby blues is greater than a typical expectant mother. Baby blues can be caused by hormonal changes and is often brought on by fatigue and a mother's expectation of the birth itself.

...

There are ways to help reduce baby blues, including getting more rest, and making more time for yourself, but these are not always options for mothers of twins or triplets, especially at the newborn stage when these feelings are most prevalent. If you can get more sleep or get out, by all means do so whenever possible.

...

If your blues are not improving but are getting worse, there is a chance you may be suffering form Postpartum Depression (PPD). PPD is also common but has more severe symptoms than baby blues. If you cry all the time, continually feel sorry for yourself or have feelings of desperation, you probably need to seek medical attention. To read more on the subject, visit Depression After Delivery, Inc. online at *www.depressionafterdelivery.com* and *www.postpartum.org. NOTE: To read about others' struggles and triumphs, purchase* The Mother-to-Mother Postpartum Depression Support *book by Sandra Poulin.*

...

If you are feeling depressed or desperate, the worst thing you can do is not share your feelings with someone. Talk to someone you can confide in, and if they suggest that you might need help, listen to them. Postpartum

Depression is treatable: Admit your feelings, don't be embarrassed by them, and get help.

• • •

I know many women who have sought professional help to get through some difficult early stages of motherhood. When I attended a mothers of multiples group meeting about a year ago, about one third of the women admitted to taking prescription drugs, and *all* of them admitted to having some form of baby blues (myself included). This is something that is real and very common in mothers of newborn twins and triplets. If you are feeling this way, realize that you are part of an overwhelming majority.

• • •

If your mood is not improving and you think you might be suffering from Postpartum Depression, don't spend another day feeling unhappy. Realize that your depression doesn't just affect you; it affects your life as well as the lives of those you love. Take control and get help. There is a reason why antidepressant drugs are a multi-billion dollar business: people need them, doctors prescribe them, and they are effective!

"Now that my kids are a little older, I am a happy person again!
When things get difficult, realize it will get easier.
I had difficulty believing this when my babies were newborns."
— Shari L. (Mother of 16-month-old BG twins)

BOUTS OF RELAXATION

Shortly after you give birth, visit a spa or salon and take an afternoon to renew yourself. Feeling like a "new" person can be a great way to start a very different phase of your life.

• • •

Use your glider or rocking chair and take some time to rock yourself every now and then. Do this with your favorite cup of coffee or tea, or even a favorite glass of wine. *NOTE: If you are breastfeeding, you will probably want to find something else to sip on.*

• • •

Meet a friend for a drink or cup of coffee. Getting out of the house and talking to a friend can be a real pick-me-up. If a friend can't go, go alone.

• • •

Learn to *walk* whenever your children want something. Running will exhaust you, and will cause your children to become impatient. With multiple requests, patience really is a virtue, especially for Mom!

• • •

Vent. Don't hold things inside. B-tch, complain, whine, or go into another room and scream at the top of your lungs if you have to (all mothers of multiples are known to do this from time to time!). Being open about your feelings is much healthier than keeping everything locked inside. You will find that venting really helps to relieve stress.

• • •

I don't know where I heard this, but I give credit to whoever said it: "If you win the rat race, you're still a rat!" How true is that? Try not to get caught up in it.

• • •

Be a satisfied realist, not a frustrated idealist.

• • •

Not two or three, but one thing at a time! Keep reminding yourself of this.

• • •

Thoroughly enjoy the sound of silence whenever you hear it. Once you've enjoyed it for a moment or two, think about how lonely it would be if you heard it all the time.

"I started writing a journal as a way to relax —
I had gone into pre-term labor at 28 weeks gestation.
When my boys were born prematurely (at 29 weeks), I used the
journal to record and document everything about them. In some ways, writing all of this
down helped me get through some of the rough and tough times. Every so often, I read past
entries, and the emotions tied to that day feel as fresh now as they did then. It is amazing
and comforting to know that things really do get better with time, and challenges in
the beginning can be overcome and are constantly being replaced with new ones.
Looking at them now, it is hard to believe they were just a bit longer than a ruler at birth.
I still record the special and not-so-special moments in their lives. I hope someday to share
this journal with my boys — my own way of showing how much I love them."
— Melissa B. (Mother of almost 3-year-old BB twins)

"Moms should set aside a little time everyday to work on a personal project, preferably
non-child related. This should be a project where they could see some progress being
made from day to day (photo albums, needlework, sewing, etc.) This definitely helped
my sanity and it still does!" — Kathleen H. (Mother of 5-year-old GBB triplets)

• •

SHOWERING:
THE LOGISTICAL NIGHTMARE

After your bundles of joy arrive, you will find that many of the things you took for granted will become luxuries. Taking a shower is one of them. A coworker of mine inspired me to add this section. She is a new mother who came in to the office one day shortly after her maternity leave and asked, "Can you offer any advice on how to take a shower? I can't figure out how!"

* * *

Not only do showers become a luxury, many parents have great difficulty showering once their children are born. Sound silly? Not really! If your timing isn't right, taking one can be a logistical nightmare as you try to juggle wailing and flailing infants who could care less about your hygiene.

•••

The obvious solution to showering would be to take one at night after your babies go to sleep. Although this sounds like common sense, it may not be so sensible after all, for the following reasons: 1) During the first several months, it will be anyone's guess as to what time of night your babies will fall asleep; 2) Many mothers end up pouring themselves into bed and skipping the shower at night; and 3) Most feel the need to shower in the morning because it helps them to rejuvenate.

•••

Another option is to wait until your babies go down for their first nap in the morning, but this is not as easy as it sounds! If you plan to shower during naps, first realize that newborns (and more than one of them) are not at all predictable with their sleep patterns, and having any luck showering while they sleep might be very difficult. You might have more luck once they are on a schedule, but since the majority of babies wake between 5:30 a.m. and 6:30 a.m. and don't nap until about 10 a.m., you will need to wait several hours to take your shower! Another issue: Many mothers don't like to shower during naptimes because it takes away from their window of opportunity to tackle other chores around the house.

•••

If you can't seem to find a quiet opportunity to shower, consider placing your babies safely in their cribs for a few minutes with some form of entertainment. If you do this, plan to take the quickest shower possible. You can bet money that your babies will begin to cry out of boredom after a few minutes.

•••

If you don't have it in you to let them cry for a few minutes, strap your multiples into their infant car seats (so they don't move) and put them next to the shower so they can see and hear you. As long as you are in view, they should be entertained for a good portion of your shower before getting bored. I found this worked best for me.

•••

Invest in a shower cap. You will frequently find the need to shower, but won't have the time, or possibly the desire, to wash your hair. When this happens it is a sure sign that you are close to being inducted into the

"Pony Tail and Sweatpants Club" that we all swore we would never join! Whether we like it or not, all mothers of multiples become members of this elite club, to one extent or another.

• • •

When you're really pressed for time, or if your children are simply not offering you an opportunity to shower, you can always take a "military shower." Just add deodorant and you're good to go!

• • •

About a week after our showering discussion, my coworker came in one morning and said, "Thanks for the tips on showering. Now can you tell me how to go to the bathroom without being interrupted?" After we both had a laugh, we realized that the things we took for granted truly are luxuries once we become mothers. As far as bathroom advice goes, I think some things are better left unsaid! I will make mention of one thing: No matter how rushed you are, take a moment to close the bathroom door. If you're not sure why, just ask my neighbor!

"I found what worked best for me was setting my alarm clock to go off about fifteen minutes before my twins would normally wake up (about 5:45 a.m.). Even though it was early, I found it was the only time I could take a shower without washing and pulling my hair out at the same time. If I waited until the last minute, it would throw my entire morning off." — A mother who loves her showers and twin boys.

"Whenever you take a shower, try to relax as best as you can, but be careful not to get too comfortable, and don't even think about taking a bath!"
— Linda O. (Mother of BG twins)

BATHING YOUR BEAUTIES

D on't add to your workload by thinking you need to bathe your babies every day. You can save yourself lots of time by making use of a warm soapy washcloth instead of a bathtub. *NOTE: When you first bring your newborns home, plan to bathe them in the kitchen sink. This should be easier when you are trying to recuperate for the first several weeks.*

• • •

Some good news for new parents: Newborn babies don't have to have their hair washed until they are about six weeks old. In fact, washing an infant's hair too often can cause dry skin and an itchy scalp. Focus on mastering how to clean other parts, like the belly button and other challenging crevices, before putting yourself to the ultimate test of trying to keep soap out of their eyes.

• • •

If you plan to bathe infants together, don't do it alone — the hazards far outweigh the time you will save in the bathroom. Potential dangers are magnified with multiples, and a child can drown in the time it takes to run for a towel.

• • •

Multiple babies in a tub can create their own chaos. They kick, splash, scream, most often in fun, but without help, their fun can be dangerous. If you add a frazzled parent to the mix, you have an accident waiting to happen. If you must bathe your little ones without help, put the other(s) in a safe place and bathe them individually. Unless they both/all ended up in a pigpen together, consider bathing them on different days or nights of the week.

• • •

Bathing multiples can be quite an undertaking and can be very time consuming. Don't prolong the process. Keep toys in the bath to a minimum. Too many toys are often the cause of disagreements about getting out of the bathtub. Get your babies in, get them washed, and get them out. If they want to play, let them do it in a safe place other than a slippery bathtub.

• • •

If you have time and someone to help you, it is certainly acceptable to let kids be kids. Let your babies have fun and splash in the bath for a while as long as their fun is not getting out of control.

• • •

When you bathe your babies, put a minimal amount of water in the bathtub. With children in the bath and too much water, the entire bathroom, including parents, will end up soaked! If you've created your own indoor water park, plan to take as much time mopping up as you do bathing. If need be, wear an apron to protect yourself from splashes.

• • •

If you bathe more than one child at a time, you will need all the elbowroom you can get. If you have a designated "kids only" bathroom, remove the shower curtain to unclutter the space and allow yourself more room for bathing.

• • •

Protective faucet covers are a must with multiples in the bath. If you can find them, buy inflatable covers. They seemed to stay in place better than rubber and are more difficult to pull off.

• • •

Johnson & Johnson has a handy product on the market called "Head-to-Toe" baby wash, which is perfect for shampooing and bathing multiples. It is an all-in-one product you can use instead of fumbling for different soap bottles. You can find this soap just about any place baby items are sold, including grocery stores.

• • •

Once multiples outgrow their bathtubs, shop around for the largest bath mat you can find. If you can't find anything larger than a standard size, look for one at *www.perfectlysafe.com*. They sell an extra large bath mat for about $20.

BEDTIME BASICS

Put layers of clothing, not blankets, on your infants for warmth when you put them to bed at night. Also, be careful not to overheat your babies. This is thought to increase the risk of SIDS (Sudden Infant Death Syndrome).

•••

Controlling when newborns call it a night is close to impossible. Since their sleep patterns are erratic and they don't understand a word, don't expect to have any say in their bedtime for months. Sleep is not something you can force your newborns into.

•••

You might find that one of your newborns sleeps for 4 hours while another sleeps for a mere 10 minutes. On the next round of naps, the 4-hour napper might take a 20-minute nap while his sibling takes a 3-hour nap. Three hours might later turn into 10 minutes, and the 20-minute napper might sleep or be up the remainder of the day, and vice versa! Does this make any sense? It shouldn't, and it won't for the first few months!

•••

Don't expect because "newborns sleep most of the day" that you will be able to get some much-needed rest during this time. Prepare to be up late for the first few months and up most of your days as well. Parents of twins or triplets find the newborn stage to be exceptionally difficult. It is not uncommon to find them up at midnight, or even later, as they wait for the "last man standing" to fall asleep. By the time this happens, parents have more than likely survived "the witching hours" (hours of continuous crying) and gone through every relaxation technique they can muster to get their babies to settle down.

•••

Although there isn't much one can do about infant sleep patterns, one thing that helps is to find a comfortable room to relax in, and prepare your babies by creating a sleep atmosphere. This will involve much more than placing your babies in their cribs and turning out the lights! Dimming the lights, turning down the volume on the television, talking softly, putting your babies in comfortable nightwear, and rocking them are excellent ways to start the bedtime process.

•••

At nighttime, the best way to handle the unexpected is to be flexible. One single technique used to prepare your babies for sleep will not necessarily work for all babies, nor is it guaranteed to work every night for the same baby. Try several approaches to soothe and relax your babies, and when you find something that works, try it again the following night.

•••

Gently rock them, swing them, offer a bouncy seat, sing to them, hold and cuddle them, pat their backs or bottoms, massage them, walk with them, gently tickle their faces — do everything you can to relax them enough for one last feeding. After they've had their last feeding at night, there is a good chance they will fall asleep.

•••

If need be, "let sleeping dogs lie." If your babies have a habit of waking whenever you try to move them into their cribs at night, it may make sense not to move them. Many parents of multiples let their babies sleep in infant car seats, bouncy seats, and even swings. Do whatever you can (and whatever you feel comfortable with), to simplify the process whenever possible.

• • •

Don't make the mistake of trying to keep your babies awake all day, assuming they will sleep at night. This will not work. What they do during the day will have little correlation to what they do at night, at least during the infant stage. You will also find that you have good nights and not-so-good nights. A good night is when your babies feed and go right back to sleep and a not-so-good night is when babies feed and are up for hours following a feeding.

• • •

After your babies are on a schedule (6+ months), establish a predictable, regimented bedtime routine. Being consistent will be the key to getting them to bed, and to sleep, at a reasonable hour for years to come.

SLEEPING: CHILDREN AND PARENTS

The latest thinking is that babies should be put to sleep on their backs to help reduce the risk of Sudden Infant Death Syndrome (SIDS). According to the *Archives of Pediatrics & Adolescent Medicine*, research has showed that "back-to-sleep" babies were significantly less likely to have trouble sleeping, develop fevers, or have stuffy noses. Another note: Some mothers have worried that a baby on her back would choke if she vomited in her sleep. This study (which involved thousands of babies under six months of age) found no evidence of this being a danger. *NOTE: "Sleep positioners" assure that babies stay in their "back to sleep" positions at night. Babies are also less likely to disturb their cribmate(s) when sleeping in them.*

• • •

According to the Consumer Product Safety Commission (CPSC), you should not allow any child younger than two years of age to sleep in your bed with you at night. Without a doubt, it's easier to stop a baby from crying by allowing him to sleep with you, but if you do, you are putting your child at risk of suffocation.

• • •

You might think it will be easier to get more sleep if you let your newborns sleep in your bedroom with you at night. Words of wisdom: If you do this, no one will sleep! Use a monitor and keep them as far away from your room as possible, but not so far that you will not be able to hear a cry for a bottle.

• • •

Infants often make more noises while asleep than awake. When multiples sleep, it can sound like being in a forest in the middle of the night — they make strange sounds. When you hear something that sounds like a hungry bear, it's more than likely feeding time again! This is yet another reason to keep them out of your bedroom at night.

• • •

If you have a nursery that affords you the space, consider keeping your multiples in the same room. It will save you time running from room to room, especially at night. Keeping them together will also give you a few extra minutes in the morning once they begin to interact with one another. Many parents also choose to keep their babies in the same crib in the early months. Having a close physical contact with a sibling(s) tends to calm newborns and make them sleep better.

• • •

It will be easy to feel sorry for yourself as you sit exhausted at night feeding and attending to babies. The worst part is, it seems just when you lay your head down, it's time to make the donuts again! Within reason, it is perfectly normal to feel this way. When this happens, remember that the newborn stage is very brief, and be thankful you don't have septuplets!

• • •

Share the work at night! Don't become one of those mothers who wakes every night to feed her babies because "your husband has to work in the morning." Keep this in mind: Caring for multiples is not like caring for one child, and it can be a lot more work than a desk job with coffee breaks. Unless your spouse truly requires sleep in order to perform well or to be safe on his job, don't accept "going to work" as an excuse. If you do, you will be sorry!

• • •

Take turns at night. If you and your spouse wake at night for every feeding, the interrupted sleep will quickly get the best of both of you. Consider switching nights with your spouse (one night on, one night off), or splitting nights (i.e., wife feeds until 2 a.m., husband feeds between 2 a.m. and 6 a.m.). *NOTE: If you are breastfeeding, this schedule may not work unless you supplement or pump your breastmilk.*

• • •

Wait for your babies to tell you they are hungry at night; don't set an alarm clock to tell you, unless there is a health or nutrition issue. You will have difficulty waking your babies if you do this and much more difficulty getting any rest.

• • •

When your first hungry baby wakes to feed at night, wake the other(s) at the same time and consider propping bottles to simultaneously feed them. Get feedings over and done with at night, and get back to sleep while the opportunity exists. *NOTE: If you breastfeed, do your best to nurse two at a time.*

• • •

If you bottle feed, save yourself trips to the kitchen at night. Pack chilled bottles in a cooler and bring it into your bedroom, or put them in a small refrigerator in your bathroom. When your babies wake, warm the bottles under hot running water to take the chill out of them.

• • •

For bottle feeders, put an infant car seat in your babies' nursery at night (or two if you have triplets). When you feed at night, hold and feed one baby as you prop bottles to feed the other(s) in their car seats. Infant car seats are perfect for propping bottles because the seats recline to a 45-degree angle. This holds a head up enough for feeding and the raised edge of the seat keeps your "propping device" in place. *NOTE: Boppy pillows and bouncy seats will also suffice.*

• • •

Put a night-light in the nursery or use a dimmer switch when you feed in the middle of the night. Turning on a harsh light can wreak havoc. Wake your infants gradually and avoid startling them.

...

Avoid speaking to your infants while feeding them in the wee hours of the night. Talking to them is a wonderful thing, but not at 3 a.m.!

...

If a baby won't go back to sleep at night after a feeding, try putting him in a mechanical swing. If a swing doesn't lull him back to sleep, try a vibrating bouncy seat, or as a last resort, rock him.

...

One major factor in getting infants to sleep through the night is their weight. Don't expect your babies to sleep through the night until they weigh at least 10 pounds. Nothing you do will get them to sleep through the night until they are at least this size (if not more). Know this going into it, accept it, and save yourself aggravation trying to get them to sleep before they reach this weight.

...

If you give birth to preemies, don't compare your babies' sleep patterns to other full term babies. I recall a late-night phone call from a friend who called me in tears because her seven-month-old triplets were not sleeping through the night. She asked for my advice and I quickly had an answer for her: Give it more time! They were not sleeping through the night because her once two-pound babies were still too small and in need of food at night. Her problem had nothing to do with sleep training.

...

You may have heard the old wives tale that you should put rice cereal in your babies' bottles to make them sleep better at night. Don't be too optimistic if you try this. You will probably find it doesn't do much of anything, other than make a mess as your babies gag from the faster formula flow (you will have to cut a larger hole in the bottle nipple). If you believe in wives tales, give it a try, but be sure to check with your pediatrician first.

...

When you hear a cry for a bottle or a cry that may indicate something is "not right," don't hesitate to attend to your babies at night. If you hear anything else, do your best to ignore it (this is much easier said than done!). Babies often wake for no apparent reason at night. The best thing to do is to let them find a way to calm themselves enough to fall back to sleep on their own. Babies will need to learn to settle themselves before they will be able to sleep through the night.

• • •

Once your babies have gained weight and begin to sleep for longer periods of time, pass up on changing their diapers at night unless you have no choice. Put them in "premium" or "supreme" diapers at night at this stage. These diapers do a fantastic job with keeping babies dry, and they also promote sleeping!

• • •

When the time comes to pass up on changing diapers at night, pass up on waking them to feed as well. Feed only the baby who wakes for a bottle. Let the other(s) sleep as long as possible. Your focus will switch from feeding as much as possible, to getting them to sleep as much as possible at night.

• • •

Be cautious of the fact that "sleeping through the night" means different things to different people. Most consider midnight to 5 or 6 a.m. sleeping through the night. When your babies grow older, sleeping through the night could very well mean 7 p.m. through 6 a.m.! Sleeping through the night could also mean one night, or several nights in a row. Be aware of this when someone boasts that "Little Johnny" is sleeping through the night at eight weeks of age. You may be comparing apples and oranges.

• • •

Don't expect your multiples to begin sleeping through the night at the same time. As an example, one of my sons began to consistently sleep through the night at four months, and my other two did not sleep through the night until six months of age. The son to sleep through the night sooner was the largest at birth, drank much more formula, and gained weight much sooner than my other two.

• • •

There is no magic "sleep training" technique that you should follow to get your babies to sleep through the night. Your goal should be to feed your babies as often and as much as possible until they are a certain size and weight (10+ lbs.). You can buy sleep-training books if you think they might help, but you will likely find the key to getting your babies to sleep through the night is nothing more than a feeding and waiting game. In the interim, focus on your own sleep training!

• • •

If a child suddenly begins waking again after months of consistently sleeping through the night, he is probably teething. Another reason for waking could be an ear infection, or some other ailment. If a child seems unusually irritable and is not sleeping, schedule an appointment with the pediatrician to determine the cause.

• • •

"Sleep when they sleep." What a great concept! Taking naps is easier said than done with multiples. You will probably find a rare opportunity to nap during the day, and when you do, instead of sleeping, you will probably start thinking about all the chores you need to attend to. Take time to rest whenever possible, but don't expect to take naps too often.

• • •

Stop visitors from waking your nappers. Put a "Please Knock" sign on your front door and make sure it's large enough so people don't over-look it.

• • •

Spend quality time watching them sleep. This will make your day's challenges worthwhile.

"Make up cribs with multiple layers (sheet, waterproof pad, sheet, waterproof pad). When accidents happen in the middle of the night, take off one layer and you're ready to go, and the sheet is warm." — Andrea F. (Mother of BGB triplets)

SECRETS TO KEEP FROM YOUR SPOUSE

Pretend to be sleeping when your babies wake at night. If you do, your spouse will sooner or later give in. *NOTE: This will not work if your spouse has the same idea!*

• • •

For mothers of triplets: If both you and your spouse both wake to feed your babies at night, go straight to your slowest eater and offer a bottle. When your husband's baby finishes first, it only makes sense that he has to feed the third baby. As he begins to feed the third baby, quickly finish feeding yours, and get back to sleep!

• • •

If it is your night to feed, complain of a headache before getting into bed. When the babies wake to be fed, tell your spouse your headache is "unbearable" and ask if he "wouldn't mind" helping you. Offer him a weakened kiss as he drags himself out of bed.

• • •

These secrets have obviously been included in this manual for fun, but it might be helpful to note that they are real wife-tested tactics that work! Give them a try, but don't expect to be able to get away with using them for very long!

CRIBS AND BEDS

Plenty of infants can literally scream into each other's ears without waking one another while sharing a crib. On the other hand, some parents find this is not the case, as they separate their multiples into different cribs and sometimes bedrooms as a result. For convenience sake, try keeping yours together to start. If you find that they wake each other, first try separate cribs, and then bedrooms if necessary.

• • •

Twins, and even triplets, can share the same crib from birth to about six months of age (it depends on the babies). When they begin to move around freely and invade each other's space, it will be time to think about moving them into their own cribs. *NOTE: Some parents keep their babies together in the same crib for up to 18 months or even longer, although this is not common. ANOTHER NOTE: You can prolong crib sharing by purchasing a crib divider online at* www.doubleblessings.com. *(Retail price: $30)*

• • •

If you use second-hand cribs, be sure they meet current safety standards and that all the parts are fastened tightly and that none are missing. I used "almost new" cribs, and my son got his head caught between two pieces of the crib that had come apart. If I hadn't been using a monitor during his nap, it could have resulted in a tragedy. Grab that screwdriver, and fasten those screws as tightly as possible! Be sure to do this with new cribs as well. *NOTE: A safe crib should have slats that are no wider than 2⅜", a mattress no greater than 5" in depth, and you should not be able to fit more than 4 fingers between the mattress and the side of the crib.*

• • •

Think about putting one crib upstairs and one downstairs in your home for the first several months. It can be downright exhausting carrying multiples up and down stairs for naps, especially as they continue to gain weight. Having cribs in different locations can also come in handy if you have night help and want to get some peaceful sleep. Sleep upstairs while your help takes care of babies downstairs. *NOTE: A formal dining room, or other quiet, relatively dark, room is perfect for placing a second crib (put both/all of your babies to sleep in it).*

• • •

Use "crib tents" once your children make an attempt to climb out of their cribs. Kids like them, and they often ask to be zipped in! Before you purchase two or three of them, shop around because their prices vary considerably. I have seen them range in price from the high $40s to the high $80s (Babies "R" Us offers them at a reasonable price). My children used crib tents for more than a year, which meant lots of quality sleep for me! *NOTE: Visit the manufacturer, Tots in Mind* (www.totsinmind.com) *for a retailer in your area.*

• • •

Keep your children in their cribs as long as possible. You enter a whole new world of challenges when they start sleeping in a bed.

TIPS TO DIGEST: SOLID FOOD

Most babies are ready to start eating solid foods between the ages of four and six months, although this is not always the case, particularly with babies who are born prematurely. Offering solid foods too soon can be hurtful to little digestive systems, and can cause babies to choke if they are not mature enough to handle them. Be sure to get permission from your pediatrician before introducing solid food.

• • •

The first solid food babies typically eat is one or two tablespoons of dry rice cereal mixed with formula or breast milk. If babies don't show signs of a food intolerance, they later graduate to thicker cereals, then fruits, vegetables, and finally, meats. *NOTE: There are certain foods that are known to cause an allergic reaction in many children. Some very common ones are nuts, citrus, shellfish, and dairy products. Get permission before offering any of these!*

•••

When you first introduce solids you might find that one eats as if he's been eating for years as another spits his food out. Although you may get some resistance, be persistent and continue to offer solids to each child until he or she gets the hang of it. Don't expect the first week or two of feeding to be easy, and don't expect it be anything less than hysterical. Don't forget bibs and your camera!

•••

Buy three or four rubber-coated baby spoons per child. They make feedings easier on gums and teeth.

•••

Buy four small plastic bowls for each child for feedings. Or, if you're like the majority of mothers of twins or more, buy a few more that aren't so small that can hold enough food for everyone. To save time, feed from the same bowl (unless someone is sick).

•••

When you first shop for jars or containers of fruits and vegetables (after your babies have had success with dry cereal), buy flavors in small quantities. You may discover that your babies do not like it, and you'll find yourself eating pureed prunes for lunch for the next month!

•••

Before you stock up on baby food, check with the grocery store manager to find out when they are scheduled to go on sale. Baby food is often on sale and you can save lots of money if your timing is right.

•••

If you want to get even with a grocery store cashier because she overcharged you on your last visit, stock up on individual jars of baby food! Kidding aside, when you opt to buy individual jars of baby food, it can be a real inconvenience, not just for the cashier, but for you as well. Look to buy them in 4 packs or by the case whenever possible (after you know your babies will eat it).

•••

Be careful not to stock up on baby food as your babies approach the "Stage 3" baby food (about nine+ months). You might be surprised to find that your hungry herd suddenly refuses to eat it. As this age approaches, start to bring your inventory levels down, or you may end up with an entire pantry full of baby food that nobody wants.

• • •

If you have twins, expect that your duo will devour about 1,200 jars of baby food within a five-month period, with triplets; give or take 1,800! With twins, plan to spend about $576 on jars of baby food, and with triplets, about $864. *NOTE: This is an approximate consumption cost for jars of baby food and does not include everything else they will snack on! ANOTHER NOTE: If you choose to prepare homemade baby food, expect to save money. It's often cheaper and usually contains more nutrients than store-bought baby food.*

• • •

For more information or ideas about what to feed your little ones, look for a book entitled, the *Super Baby Food Book*, by Ruth Yaron. This book was featured on "Good Morning America," and can be found online at *www.amazon.com.*

THE INFAMOUS "SCHEDULE"

I have yet to meet a mother of multiples who has truly had her babies on a schedule much before six months of age. Accept that a schedule will probably not happen for at least six months, and understand that it could take much longer. This will primarily depend on the birth weights and age of your infants. *NOTE: A schedule will not happen until sometime after your babies are consistently sleeping through the night.*

• • •

A "schedule" just seems to happen, and when it does, it will be obvious. Your babies will begin to do things, such as become tired or hungry, at very predicable times of the day on a regular basis. A "schedule" means you will be reacting to what they are doing, *not* that they will be reacting to what you are doing. Don't waste your energy trying to get a schedule to work. It will, when your babies are ready!

...

Once a predictable pattern for each child is established, the challenge will be to get both or all of your babies on the same schedule. If you stay focused on doing as much as possible on a group basis (accepting that it won't happen every time to start), you will succeed. As an example, if you find that Baby A is always ready for a nap at 9 a.m., and Baby B is not ready until 10 a.m., start putting them down at the same time at 9:30 a.m.

...

When you do everything as a group, you will need to put your babies to sleep while they are awake. Be sure to do this for naps as well as bedtime in order to achieve synchronized sleep patterns. If you have one baby who requires lots of sleep and another who does not, continue to put them to bed at the same time. You will find that they will nap together, but possibly not for the same length of time.

...

Although you should plan to put your babies to sleep at the same time, you should no longer wake them at the same time as you did when they were newborns. Allow each of them to sleep and wake when they are good and ready. Doing this should not throw off your routine. If one wakes sooner, enjoy some one-on-one time with this child.

...

Some mothers choose *not* to put their children to sleep at the same time. They find it easier to attend to one child while the other(s) sleeps. If you find this to be the case, understand that there is no real need to put your children to sleep at the same time, unless your goal is to establish a synchronized daily routine.

...

If you establish a synchronized schedule, you will be able to predict what your babies will do almost down to the minute! When this happens, take a few minutes to put together a schedule of what they do throughout the day. This will help you as well as others who take care of them. Place the chart somewhere in your kitchen where others can refer to it. *Your schedule might look something like this:*

SAMPLE DAILY SCHEDULE	
6:30	Wake Time
6:45	Diapers
7:00	Breakfast
9:30	Bottles
9:45	Morning Nap
11:45	Diapers
12:00	Lunch
2:00	Snack
2:15	Diapers
2:30	Afternoon Nap
4:15	Diapers
5:00	Dinner
6:15	Diapers
6:45	Bottles
7:00	Bedtime

• • •

When your multiples are on a schedule, stick to their schedule. Don't plan to go out during nap times and expect them to be awake and happy. Venture out after naps, when they are refreshed. It will make your day with them much more enjoyable and productive.

• • •

Schedules can make parents' lives easier and they can complicate them as well. You will find your children's schedule will dictate everything you do, or don't do.

• • •

Most babies start out their schedules by taking one morning and one afternoon nap. Before long your children will outgrow one of their naps (usually the morning nap). When this happens, it will allow you to be more flexible with activities you have planned for the day.

• • •

When a schedule is established, get into the habit of putting your babies to bed at night at a reasonable hour. If you do, you may find that you suddenly have a life after 7 p.m.! At this point, sleeping through the night should mean 7 p.m. to 6 a.m., not midnight to 5 or 6 a.m.

ONE-ON-ONE TIME

A child always enjoys one-on-one time with Mom or Dad, no matter what he is doing. Find as many opportunities as possible to spend time on an individual basis with each child. Family time is also nice, but realize there will be occasions when it won't be practical for everyone to go shopping for a bag of nails at Home Depot! This type of outing is perfect for one-on-one time.

...

If you plan to spend one-on-one time with a child, be prepared to deal with crying as you leave with the "Chosen One." Be sure the one(s) staying home has something special to do; anything from baking cookies to visiting a neighbor.

...

Extra special one-on-one time is any time spent with a grandparent. Not only can grandparents be fun to be around, they can also be a tremendous help to parents. When grandparents ask to spend time with their grandchildren, you might suggest that they take one child for a few hours or even overnight. This could be a win-win situation for everyone.

NOTE: If grandparents plan to care for more than one child at a time, they should consider caring for them in the children's home. This is usually easier for everyone. ANOTHER NOTE: See THINGS TO CONSIDER/ THINGS TO AVOID for a list of grandparent essentials.

• • •

One-on-one time does not mean that you must leave your house with one baby. Take some time to talk to each one of your children before you kiss them good night. This may be one of the few individual conversations you will have with them all day. Their conversation with you will be the last thing they remember before they fall asleep.

• • •

Consider "none-on-one" time every now and then. Sometimes it's best to leave your children at home with your spouse or babysitter and go out alone. This can be productive as well as relaxing!

COMPARISONS

There is a natural tendency to compare multiples. My twin and I were well aware of our strengths and weaknesses because other people told us about them! If you want to discourage sibling rivalry, avoid openly comparing your children.

• • •

Avoid comparing your children in such a way that it might hurt them. Saying something as harmless as "Child A is the shy one," can damage self-esteem and might magnify problems or competition with siblings.

• • •

Never admit in front of your children that you have a "favorite" and don't ever joke about it!

• • •

"You should never compare multiples" is true in a general sense, in that every child is an individual. However, if your intuition tells you there may be a developmental or medical issue with one or more of your children, don't delay in seeking a professional's opinion. Multiple birth children have a much higher rate of developmental delays and medical issues compared to singletons.

• • •

Speak slowly and clearly, and allow your children to see your face whenever you speak. Multiple birth children have a higher rate of speech delays than singletons and speaking in this way will help your babies to develop speech and language skills.

• • •

If you suspect that there may be a developmental issue with any of your children, share your thoughts with your child(ren)'s pediatrician, or contact the hospital where your babies were born to see if it offers a neonatal development follow-up program. Many Level III hospitals offer this program to former patients.

• • •

One great advantage to having multiples is that you *can* compare them. Parents of multiples usually identify potential problems much sooner than parents of singletons, who might otherwise think their child is developing at a normal pace.

"If you think there is something developmentally 'not quite right' with your children, you are probably right. Even if pediatricians do not take your concerns seriously, you should get in touch with an early intervention program to get an evaluation. If you are wrong, you can put your mind at rest. If there is something going on, you may very well be able to catch it early so that it will not impact your child's education later. If nothing else, you may get some good exercises to use with your child." — Randi C. (Mother of 2½-year-old BG twins)

CREATIVE GROCERY SHOPPING

Someone once sent me an e-mail full of analogies. One of them suggested that grocery shopping with a young child is like "trying to control a wild goat that got loose in a vegetable aisle." If this was the analogy for one child, can you imagine what it's like trying to control more than one? Realize what you are in for if you plan to grocery shop with your kids (aren't "kids" baby goats?).

• • •

Grocery stores were not built for mothers of multiples nor were their carts. Their baby products tend to be more expensive, and their carts don't accommodate more than one infant. If you have to bring more than one infant grocery shopping, don't go alone. Unless you have quadruplets…I know a woman who goes grocery shopping, alone, with her three-year-old daughter and six-month-old quadruplets! She told me she puts her older child in the grocery cart seat, pushes the cart, and pulls the quad stroller behind her. I once laughed and (half) jokingly told her she was a glutton for punishment. She disagreed and told me, "I'm actually a genius! Every time I go grocery shopping everyone in the store offers to help!"

• • •

Whenever possible, shop without your children at night, on weekends, or whenever your spouse is available. This will give you time to think, smell the fresh-ground coffee in aisle nine, use coupons, and stock up on groceries.

• • •

If your grocery store has a "baby club," take a minute to join. Some stores offer baby clubs that are money-saving incentives for customers to buy its baby products. Even if a club is not advertised, inquire about it. There will be plenty of times when you will shop for baby products in grocery stores, primarily out of convenience.

• • •

Avoid shopping for diapers in a grocery store unless they are on sale. If you stack all of the diapers you will need in your cart, there will be no room left for anything else. Even if you were an expert "Jenga" player in your day, you may be able to stack a few on top of your groceries, but don't count on it. *NOTE: If you find a sale on diapers, load up your cart and remember to use coupons in combination with your purchase. If you find a significant savings, consider purchasing larger diapers that your children will grow into.*

• • •

Some grocery stores offer free on-site babysitting services while you shop. You might have to travel out of your neighborhood to take advantage of this, but if you manage to locate one, it will be worth your while.

"It's such a hassle to go out for a head of lettuce! Don't expect to be able to 'run out' to the grocery store anymore." — Laura S. (Mother of 8-month-old GGG triplets)

SHOPPING:
SAVING MONEY AND YOUR SANITY

Avoid shopping by learning to love hand-me-downs. If you don't already, you will!

...

Befriend a mother of multiples who has children one to two years older than yours and ask if she would be willing to sell her children's' clothing at a reduced price. This past spring I asked a friend if I could buy clothing that her children had outgrown. She agreed, and I packed my children's closets full of beautiful summer outfits for $125. I'm sure the value was well over $500. The outfits were in perfect condition and all top quality.

...

Look to the Internet and catalogs as convenient alternatives to mall shopping. Not only is mall shopping a test of one's patience, preparing to go can be a chore in and of itself.

...

The following is a list of some favorite catalogs that I (and many others) have used that are great for parents with small children:

Clothing:
Hanna Andersson *(www.hannaandersson.com)* — (800) 222-0544
The Wooden Soldier *(www.woodensoldierltd.com)* — (800) 375-6002

Crib Bedding & Accessories:
Land of Nod *(www.landofnod.com)* — (800) 933-9904
Olive Kids *(www.olivekids.com)* — (order through their website)
Pottery Barn Kids *(www.potterybarnkids.com)* — (800) 993-4923
Warm Biscuit Bedding Co. *(www.warmbiscuit.com)* — (800) 231-4231
Posh Tots *(www.poshtots.com)* — (866) POSHTOT

Safety Products:
One Step Ahead *(www.onestepahead.com)* — (800) 950-5120
Right Start *(www.rightstart.com)* — (888) 548-8531
Safety 1st *(www.safety1st.com)* — (800) 544-1108

Along with requesting a catalog, if you register as a "preferred" customer through some of these websites, you will be able to take advantage of special sales and savings.

...

When you shop with your babies, ask a friend to go with you. A friend is good company and can also serve as an extra pair of hands. A mother of triplets once shared her shopping experience with a group of mothers in one of my clubs. She told us how successful her shopping trip was until a wheel fell off of her triple stroller! Everyone got a laugh at her misfortune, and at the same time learned a valuable lesson: Bring a friend, or if you must go alone, pack a wrench in your diaper bag!

...

Buy bottle straps that connect bottles to your stroller. This will save you from losing bottles or picking them up off the floor every time someone drops or throws one. *NOTE: Visit* www.nothrow.com *to order No-Throw bottle straps. (Retail price: $5)*

• • •

Save money by shopping at mothers of multiples tag sales. Great bargains are always found for babies, and usually in excellent condition. Tag sales are perfect for mothers of twins and triplets, because just about everything for sale is sold in twos and threes. One of the best things about them is that you can resell everything you bought by getting your own table at the next sale!

• • •

Take advantage of multiples discounts. If you aren't sure if a store offers a discount, ask the sales clerk (Babies "R" Us is one of them). Although some stores might not have a formal program, you may be able to get a discount by inquiring about one. *NOTE: Buying "multiple" new outfits for yourself does not count! Multiple discounts apply if you buy at least two of the same item, which are intended for your twins or triplets. Be sure to mention this to those who shop for your baby shower and other gifts.*

• • •

Look for great baby bargains in dollar stores. I stopped in a Dollar Tree store the other day and found Gerber baby bottles, Fisher-Price spoons, Johnson's baby soap, baby shampoo, lotion, baby bowls, powdered formula dispensers, 3-packs of pacifiers, spill proof cups, bottle brushes, and lots more. I didn't find a jumbo pack of diapers for a dollar, but just about everything else!

• • •

If stores have purchase limits on particular items, be sure to explain that you have multiples, and more often than not, they will waive their limits for you (Babies "R" Us is known to do this with their diapers).

"Take some time to shop for yourself, even if you don't buy anything.
When my husband came home yesterday, I told him I was going shopping.
He asked, 'For what?' I told him, 'For nothing. I'm just going shopping!'"
— Laura S. (Mother of 8-month-old GGG triplets)

DINE AND DASH

Go out for a nice relaxing dinner, and take your last bite! Get ready to make some drastic changes in your eating and dining habits. When you eat out with your young children, it will probably be from necessity and not for leisure and enjoyment.

• • •

Unless you can find a babysitter, your fine dining days will soon be few and far between. Fine dining and multiples don't mix, no matter what their age. If they are young, they are too noisy and disruptive, and if they are older, they are too expensive!

• • •

Seek out restaurants that are kid friendly and have lots of commotion. The key to enjoying dinner out with your multiples will be whether you are successful in finding a restaurant that allows you to blend in with the frazzled masses. If people aren't pointing fingers at you or rolling their eyes, you can assume that you are welcome!

• • •

Have someone run into the restaurant to check on table availability before you take everyone out of the car. This will save you from unloading and reloading the troops if you find the wait is too long. Food, no matter how good, will not be worth waiting for if the wait is more than 10 minutes.

• • •

If one of your favorite pastimes is eating out, enjoy it while your children are infants. The infant stage, as compared to toddler and preschool, is much easier on parents for a few reasons: 1) Infants stay put; 2) They will probably sleep through your meal or most of it; and 3) They don't need a menu!

• • •

Ask your waitress for your check and pay for your meal as soon as you finish ordering your food. This gives you the freedom to leave the restaurant in a hurry, in case all "hell" breaks loose. If you linger long enough, it probably will!

• • •

Bring bottles or spill proof cups with you instead of ordering drinks for your children in a restaurant. Paying for drinks can substantially add to your bill and can turn a reasonably priced meal into an expensive one. *NOTE: If you want your children to eat their dinner, offer drinks after their meal.*

• • •

A parent of multiples dream come true is seeing a sign that says, "Kids under "X" eat free!" Take full advantage! Not only is the restaurant giving away free food, it's bound to be kid friendly.

• • •

When your babies grow into toddlers, one of your greatest challenges will be avoiding fast food restaurants. If your kids start cheering at the sight of the golden arches or start singing, "McDonalds had a Farm," it's probably time to start looking for other food options!

• • •

Don't be fooled when another mother of multiples tells you her kids have never seen the inside of a fast food restaurant. When she says this, she is probably not insinuating that they have never eaten there, but rather that they always opt for the drive through! When mothers have multiples, they find the drive-through feature irresistible, because it means they don't have to unload everyone in order to eat.

•••

When you've had your fill of quick burgers, another favorite is the local pizzeria. If you plan to dine in, order your pizza by phone before you leave the house. When you arrive, your pizza will be ready and waiting for your family. When you get to the restaurant, ask to have your pizza double cut so you don't have to do it.

•••

Don't obsess about your children's noise level in restaurants. Many times children are not as loud as you might think, and a parent is sometimes to blame for disturbing others. "Sssshhh! I said quiet! Sssshhh!" How annoying is that? Be aware of your own noise level while attempting to quiet others.

THE LAUNDRY LIST

Keep a bucket of warm water and Biz laundry detergent in your laundry room (out of reach of your children). When your babies spit up or dribble formula on themselves, apply Spray 'n Wash, and immediately soak the clothing. If you soak until you do a load of wash, you will be surprised to find the formula stains have vanished. If you allow the clothing to sit without soaking, just about everything your children wear will be stained. For impossible stains, use OXI Wash laundry detergent. You can purchase this product online at *www.tvproducts4less.com.*

• • •

You will soon have a laundry room full of "singletons"! Keep your families' stray socks in one place by purchasing a stack basket that can sit on your counter top or floor. You can find them online at Linens 'n Things *(www.lnt.com)* or any store that sells housewares. Because the baskets stack on top of one another, you will probably find use for a second or third one. Stack baskets are great organizers as well as space savers.

...

Make room for mountains of dirty clothing by purchasing a laundry basket for each child, or the largest one you can find. You will be filling them up daily.

...

If you are lucky enough to have one, ask your housekeeper to help with your children's laundry. How many times have you heard a mother with small children say, "I don't know why I pay for a cleaning lady. After fifteen minutes, you would never know she was here?" If you ask your housekeeper to spend less time tracking down every piece of dust and more time with your children's' laundry, you will be amazed at how much more helpful this becomes.

...

When you have children, it's more important to see to it that the laundry gets done than to make sure messes are picked up around the house. Before you know it, clean floors will be messy again, but the laundry pile will only get bigger! Focus on laundry first, then messes.

"Get acquainted with your laundry room. Install a phone, a television and a stereo system!"
— Carol F. (Mother of GBG triplets)

THE DIRT ON MESSES

When you obsess about a not-so-perfect home and are preoccupied with the fact that everything has a place, take a step back and realize that you and your family are the only ones who suffer.

•••

You will probably find it difficult to pick up after your children and be able to prove that you cleaned anything by the end of the day. With multiples, picking up messes is a vicious cycle. Avoid picking up during the day, and if you must straighten up, save it for the end of the day.

•••

Rather than spending time on fruitless efforts, focus on constructive things: Organize the mail, pay bills, prepare bottles, do laundry, wash dishes, prepare dinner, or anything else that might be worthwhile.

•••

If you have a two-story home and a central vacuum system, cut down your work by purchasing another vacuum hose. Because your need to vacuum will increase, so will the number of trips you make carrying a tangled hose up and down stairs. Keep one hose upstairs, and one downstairs.

•••

Unclutter your home as often and as much as you can. If you take time every day to get rid of one or two things that are no longer needed, you will find that you are much happier living in a house that is better organized.

WORKING VACATIONS

A mother of multiples is never on vacation, even when on vacation. If she manages to go somewhere without her children, she is always thinking and concerned about them. If you don't already have children, expect your future vacations to be very different from previous vacations.

· · ·

The amount of "stuff" you bring with you on vacation is inversely related to your children's age(s). The younger they are, the more you will have to pack. If you have newborns, don't expect to be able to travel light! Think of the bare essentials you will need for your trip, and plan to buy the bulk of your formula and diapers when you reach your destination. When you're on vacation and shopping, be careful not to overstock, because you won't want to have to pack everything up and bring it back on your return trip.

• • •

Most reputable hotels offer guests port-a-cribs or full-sized cribs for children. However, you should not assume that your hotel will be able to accommodate you, so call in advance to make sure the hotel has enough cribs for your family. When you arrive at the hotel, don't forget to inspect the cribs to make sure they are safe. *NOTE: If a hotel does not have enough cribs, consider a staying in a different hotel before deciding to bring a crib with you.*

• • •

Make sure the room you are staying in is large enough to accommodate the number of cribs you will need, as well as your family. Remember, you will need some walking space — this will be your temporary living quarters while you are away from home.

• • •

If you plan to visit a crowded place, such as a theme park, dress your children alike and in bright colors. It will be much easier to keep track of them this way. You might also want to wear the same color so they can easily spot you.

• • •

In my opinion, harnesses for multiples in crowded places are well worth occasional stares. For parents of multiples, losing a child in a crowd is a real possibility, because they tend to wander in different directions as soon as they start walking. *NOTE: For hands-free child harnesses specially designed for twins or triplets, shop online at* www.tommiguard.com. *(Retail price: $38.99 – twin; $49.98 – triplet)*

• • •

If you choose not to use harnesses for your children, put a piece of paper in their pockets that says, "If I am lost, please call my parent's cell phone # (XXX) XXX-XXXX. I am staying in the "XXXX" hotel. The phone number of the hotel is (XXX) XXX-XXXX." Chances are good someone may search pockets for some form of identification, or, if your children are old enough to follow simple directions, instruct them to hand the paper to a park employee who can help them.

"When I went to visit my sister last week, I didn't sit down the entire time I was there! Not only did I have to pack up an entire minivan before we left, when we arrived, I couldn't relax. There were no gates to contain them, the house was not childproofed, and my kids had difficulty sleeping because they weren't used to their surroundings. When we got home, it took them two days to get back to their routine. Next time she's coming to visit us!" — Cathy S. (Mother of 2-year-old GBG triplets)

TAKING AWAY BOTTLES AND PACIFIERS

Many people think the longer a child uses a pacifier or bottle, the more difficult it will be to take it away. This is not true! In reality, the longer you wait, the easier it will be. Most babies have a need to suck, and as they get older this need diminishes. Don't cause yourself undue stress thinking that your children will be "addicted" to bottles and/or pacifiers if you wait too long. When the time is right for you and your multiples, then it will be time to take them away.

• • •

Don't feel guilty about waiting to take away bottles or pacifiers. Waiting is perfectly acceptable, and is probably smarter with multiples. When you are outnumbered everyday, these oral fixations can be the key to maintaining your sanity.

• • •

Don't take bottles and pacifiers away at the same time, and avoid taking them away during a transition period.

• • •

Before you plan to take anything away, prepare your children. About one week prior to the big day, talk to them about what you plan to do. Do this every day for a week until the big day comes. Even if they cannot communicate with you, they should be able to understand you.

• • •

When you take away bottles or pacifiers, you might suggest that they offer them to someone they know. Physically handing them over to someone makes it easier for young children because it seems more permanent.

• • •

If your children are old enough to understand you, put a toy in a large box for each child and keep their contents a mystery. Remove their pacifiers and tell your children if they can give them up for five days, they can each have a box as a reward. If they start to cry for a pacifier, remind them of the reward. If you can get your children to go without pacifiers for five full days, they probably won't cry for them again (even if they see another child using one). This is also the case with bottles.

• • •

Some parents find it easier to remove bottles and pacifiers during the day and allow them to be used only at night for a brief period. If you do this, don't deviate from your plan, and prepare to remove them completely within a few weeks.

• • •

When the time comes, bite the bullet and don't give in! Once you've made your decision, look for every bottle or pacifier you can find in your house and physically remove them. This is a sure bet you won't change your mind, unless you have a vehicle and convenience store around the corner!

"I remember not caring if my twins were 20 years old and still drinking from a bottle. I was in no rush, because it worked for *me* (although I wouldn't dare leave the house and give them one)! Don't feel pressure from others to take away bottles if you aren't ready."
— Maureen D. (Mother of 22-year-old BG twins and a 24-year-old singleton)

SMILES FOR THE CAMERA!

Invest in a family portrait. Many parents are diligent about having their children's portraits taken but never think to include themselves in the picture. Even if you don't like to have photos taken of yourself, have one taken for your children's sake. In a few years the portrait will be priceless, particularly in the eyes of your children.

• • •

When you have portraits taken, consider a photographer who makes house calls. They are convenient and less work than going to the mall or studio for pictures, although they may be more expensive.

• • •

Find a photographer who specializes in children's photography. They have all the tools and the experience needed to get your children to crack a smile. They also seem to have more patience, which is always a plus.

• • •

Whenever you take your own pictures of your children, remember to take group and individual pictures whenever possible. Your children are individuals as much as they are multiples, and you should emphasize this in the pictures you take.

• • •

If you have identical twins or triplets, take the time to note who's who on the back of your pictures. As the years go by, there is a chance you will not be able to make a distinction. I am living proof of this. My grandfather must have taken over a thousand pictures of me with my twin sister. Since not one of them has a marking on them, just about all of them, up to the age of two, are anyone's guess as to who's who!

• • •

Make a photo album for each child. If you take a picture that happens to be one of your favorites, have extra prints made so each child can have one.

• • •

If you can't find time to put a photo album together, find a shoebox and label them by age (i.e., "birth to six months," "six months to one year"). As you develop photos, put them in the shoebox and place the latest pictures behind the last set you had printed. At a minimum, this will keep your photos organized and in chronological order.

• • •

Consider taking up a hobby that many mothers enjoy: Scrapbooking. You can do this at home, or find a group of women who get together socially to create their photo scrapbooks. If you have an interest in scrapbooking, be sure to visit *www.scrappintwins.com*. Scrappin' Twins is the only scrapbooking manufacturer dedicated to scrapbooking supplies exclusively for twins and triplets. They offer unique designs of paper, stickers, die-cuts and embellishments that will help you create adorable layouts for your multiples. Their website includes sample layouts, message boards to talk with other scrapbooking moms of multiples, tips for taking photos of your multiples, and a shopping section.

• • •

Between film and processing costs, you will soon find yourself spending bundles on picture taking. Look to a photo-processing center to develop your film (or print your own pictures). If you can wait a few days, photo-processing centers are well worth the savings of processing through the mail. Clark Color Laboratories *(www.clarkcolor.com)* is one that offers quality, reasonably priced processing. Another very popular photo processing company is Snapfish *(www.snapfish.com)*. When using Snapfish, you can also share your photos online with family and friends.

• • •

Don't forget to take time to show the world how adorable your children are! Everywhere you go, people will want to see pictures of them. Look to my website, *www.justmultiples.com* for twin and triplet brag books. Each book holds 24 (4×6 inch) pictures.

"Take pictures of your babies once a month on their birth date every month for the first year. Pick a toy, like a stuffed animal, to put in the picture. Be sure to use the same toy every month, and at the end of the year, you have a great photo record showing how much your babies grew during the first twelve months of their lives."
— Cindy M. (Owner of Scrappin' Twins and mother of 5 children
— including 1-year-old identical twin boys).

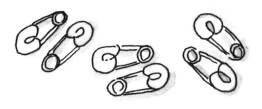

"CHILDREN" PROOFING & SAFETY

Words of wisdom: Begin the "children-proofing" and "safety" process as soon as possible. Don't wait until your house is crawling with babies and free time is limited! Review the list that follows and do as much as you can to prepare in advance. You obviously won't want to do such things as put locks on drawers before their birth, but there are plenty of preventive measures you can put in place now.

• • •

When it comes to childproofing your home, keep in mind that you will have to "children" proof your home in order to make it safe. Remember that there is strength in numbers, and you should keep your children's increased abilities in mind whenever you childproof an area of your home.

General Safety:
Consider, at the birth, to arrange for the storage of stem cells present in umbilical cord blood. These vital stem cells can be stored for a long time. Your children can in the near or distant future have access to stem cells of

their own, which may provide the key to a number of therapies. *NOTE: For more information visit* www.cyro-save.com, *or speak with your doctor.*

•••

Rent and watch an infant first aid and safety video. Watch it more than once. If you don't have luck finding one at a video store or library, inquire about one at your local firehouse. *NOTE: You can also purchase a video online at* www.amazon.com. *(Retail price: $30–35)*

•••

Take time to learn infant CPR and the Heimlich maneuver (for all ages). Classes are available through your local Red Cross. Send others for training if they will be caring for your children. If your babysitter is trained, send her for a refresher class. Keep step-by-step instructions in an obvious place to serve as a reminder in the event of an emergency. Don't take any chances! *NOTE: A video is also available, entitled, Baby & Child CPR by Dr. Kathryn Moyer and Capt. John Cappon. You can buy it online at* www.amazon.com. *(Retail price: $16.95)*

•••

Buy a large first aid kit for emergencies, bumps, and bruises. If you already have one, replace bandages and check expiration dates on medications. Keep the kit in a safe, easily accessible (to adults) location in your home.

•••

Always have a general backup plan in case of an emergency. Think of two neighbors you trust who are usually home during the day. Ask if you can call on them in the event of an emergency, and make sure they wouldn't mind a phone call in the middle of the night. Know who your contacts are ahead of time and don't be caught without a plan. You will need to know who to call in case you need to rush out of your house with one child, or alone.

•••

Put important phone numbers on your refrigerator, or some other obvious place in your kitchen. Keep an extra copy taped inside your first aid kit. These should include:

PHONE NUMBERS
- 911 (state the obvious)
- poison control

- pediatrician
- mom at work
- dad at work
- mom/dad cell
- neighbor #1
- neighbor #2
- nearby relative #1
- nearby relative #2
- other important numbers

YOUR LOCATION
10 Main Street, Apartment 3B, Anywhere, NJ

HOME PHONE
XXX-XXX-XXXX

OTHER IMPORTANT NOTES
"Child B" is allergic to XXXX

• • •

Make sure smoke alarms are working in every room and if you don't have carbon monoxide detectors, install at least one in the hallway near the bedrooms. Be sure to replace batteries twice a year so that they are all in working condition.

• • •

Have a fire evacuation plan and practice the procedure at least twice a year. Keep a fire extinguisher on every floor of your home and take a few minutes to learn how to use them.

• • •

If your house was built before 1978, have it inspected for lead paint. Lead poisoning is still a health threat to children. Call the National Lead Information Center at (800) 424-5323 for help.

• • •

Never leave a child unattended in a car. This is incredibly tempting with multiples, especially when they are sleeping. In the summer's heat, a baby can die in a matter of minutes. Sometimes wrong decisions can turn into a tragedy. Explain this to caregivers.

• • •

Nursery:

Use two furniture straps instead of one to hold tall furniture in place, or use one and connect it to a wall stud for added strength. When children work in pairs or groups, they can knock just about anything over.

• • •

Be cautious about where you place things on counter tops and dressers. Your children will use each other as step stools to reach what you assumed were "out of reach" items.

• • •

Make sure cribs are put together properly, screws are tight, and that the slats are less than 3" apart.

• • •

Do not place pillows or stuffed animals in any cribs.

• • •

Never put babies to sleep with a string pacifier attachment. Also, always remove bibs before napping or bedtime. These can cause strangulation.

• • •

Place your babies on their back when sleeping, and never sleep in the same bed with your infants.

• • •

Remove mobiles from cribs as soon as your children are able to reach them.

• • •

If the nursery is on the second level of your home, have a portable fire escape ladder readily available. Stow it under a crib so it is easy to find. Don't cram it into a cluttered closet.

Kitchen:

Keep ipecac syrup on hand (but out of reach) to induce vomiting. Have one per child in case they both/all ingest something dangerous. Keep the syrup out of reach of your children, and be sure to call poison control before you use this product! Ipecac syrup can do more damage than good if used incorrectly.

• • •

Install cabinet locks on all cabinets you don't want your children to get into. Consider using magnetic locks instead of plastic latches. The magnetic locks are a slight inconvenience because you have to find the magnetic key to unlock it, but they are better at keeping cabinets locked.

• • •

Install drawer latches to prevent children from opening drawers.

• • •

Keep large plastic bags, cleaning supplies, and sharp objects out of your children's reach.

• • •

Turn pot handles away from the edge when cooking.

• • •

Keep a fire extinguisher in your kitchen in case of a fire.

• • •

Bathroom:
Once your children become mobile, it will be impossible to watch their every move because they often run in different directions. When this happens, toilets become very dangerous. Install safety closures for your toilet lids. They are a bit of a nuisance, but safety should be your number one priority.

• • •

Never leave buckets of water anywhere (inside or outside) of your home. Children can drown within seconds in only an inch of water.

• • •

Lower the temperature in your water heater to no higher than 120 degrees Fahrenheit to avoid a potential scalding.

• • •

Install cabinet locks and drawer latches where necessary.

• • •

Place large, non-slip mats in bathtubs, and completely drain the water out of them after each use.

• • •

Keep medicines, chemicals, cleaners, and cosmetics out of reach.

• • •

Keep all electrical appliances away from water.

• • •

Living Areas:
Consider surrendering an entire room to your babies and enclose it with gates. Remove anything that could be a safety hazard and childproof the items you choose to keep in the room. Having a "safe haven" in your home will be exceptionally convenient, and best of all...safe!

...

You will need tall, sturdy gates that preferably screw into the wall for added strength (especially at the top and bottom of stairs). More than one child will test its limits by leaning or climbing on them.

...

Surround table edges with expandable table bumpers, and if you have a fireplace, use a fireplace guard.

...

Put childproof door knob covers on doors to prevent children from getting into rooms that are off limits, and if you really don't want anyone to get into a room, add a latch at the top.

...

Remove the rubber tips from doorstoppers. These are those little white rubber knobs that you find behind doors that are most often found in bathrooms and bedrooms. They are choking hazards.

...

Install plastic covers on all electric outlets that are not in use and within reach.

...

To help prevent strangulation accidents, use window-blind cord shorteners to help keep dangling cords out of reach. Use them on all windows that have dangling cords. Secure the cords up high and keep furniture away from the windows.

...

Tape wires and cords to floors and walls so no one trips or get tangled in them.

...

Choking Hazards:
Think twice before you offer your children spoonfuls of peanut butter, grapes, nuts, candy, popcorn, or hotdogs. They top the charts as the most dangerous food-related choking hazards. Share this information with other caregivers.

...

When your babies start crawling in separate directions, take extra care in sweeping and cleaning up floors. There can be lots of choking hazards for babies to get their hands on.

...

Never leave your purse on the floor! Small children are known for finding dangerous treasures in them, including medications.

...

Take potentially dangerous plants off the floor. Just about all plants can be dangerous. A child can ingest a poisonous leaf or choke on one.

...

Latex balloons are very dangerous. If they get stuck in a throat, they are often impossible to get out. If you buy balloons, purchase Mylar.

...

Additional Help/Information:

If you don't know where to begin or where to buy safety products, Perfectly Safe is a great place to start *(www.perfectlysafe.com)*. When you get to the site, it will give you childproofing ideas and products by room. *NOTE: For more products and information, visit One Step Ahead* (www.onestepahead.com) *or call (800) 950-5120, and Safety 1st* (www.safety1st.com) *or call (800) 544-1108. All of these companies offer catalogs. Request one from each company for price comparisons, easy ordering, lots of product ideas, and safety tips.*

...

For additional help in childproofing your home, buy the book, *Perfectly Safe Home* by Jeanne Miller. This book gives you room-by-room childproofing instructions and is written by a child safety expert. *(www.amazon.com)*. (Retail price: $17.95)

...

Consider hiring a professional childproofing service to do all the thinking and work for you. Look up "safety consultants" in your local phone book.

...

This is by no means an all-inclusive childproofing list. Make sure you have spent time learning as much as you can about protecting your children from potential hazards around your house.

"When figuring out how to climb out of a playpen or up a bookcase, remember that two heads are better than one. Together my boys came up with all sorts of ways to boost each other up! It pays to be cautious of this." — Sandy Y. (Mother of BB twins)

WHEN YOUR ZOO IS TWO

As your multiples get older, don't expect the amount of work involved to decrease — expect it to "change" (as you will often hear). The messes around your house can become daunting at times and the arguments and whining can seem constant. Although things may change, rest assured that parenting multiples really does get easier when your children are walking and are able to communicate.

...

Expect the level of crying to decrease and the noise level to increase during this stage. Toddlers have a way of making lots of noise and you will find yourself shouting in order to be heard. This can make talking to anyone difficult during the day.

...

Stop your children from pulling off their diapers. Dress them in overalls or buy duct tape and reinforce diapers where the tape may detach when a toddler pulls on it.

•••

Whenever practical, assign seats to avoid arguments. If you have to, assign seats for different days of the week to make things fair.

•••

Stop your toddlers from fighting over toys. Use an egg timer and set it to go off when the time comes to share. Kids will give their siblings a hard time about sharing, but they will rarely argue with an egg timer.

•••

If your car keys are missing, always look in a toy chest first. If they are not there, check the ignition, or the front door. Kids, as well as harried parents, can be blamed for missing keys. Take a minute to hang a key holder somewhere in your home.

•••

Because outings are more difficult when your kids are on the move, realize that you don't have to leave the house in order to have fun. Read to them every chance you get, teach colors, shapes, the ABCs, sing songs, and anything else you can think of.

•••

The car is a perfect classroom for multiples. When you go for a drive, take the opportunity to talk to them about their surroundings, or to teach them something new. The car is one of the few places you will have everyone's undivided attention.

•••

Children love to get mail. Multiples like to get their own mail because it is one of the few things they don't need to share with anyone. Mail each child a card, or ask grandparents or other relatives to send cards. When something arrives in the mail addressed to a child, it is often the highlight of his or her day.

•••

Instead of choosing among them, use "Eenie, Meenie, Minie, Moe" to make your decision. There is never a disagreement because it is their "law."

•••

Hide permanent markers. Although it may have taken some of the masters years to finish their great works of art, it only takes a minute with multiples!

•••

Find a drawer or cabinet in your kitchen that is large enough to hold a few toys. You will find yourself spending quite a bit of time in your kitchen, and a drawer your toddlers can call their own will be a good source of entertainment as you make quick meals. *NOTE: A drawer full of toys will prove to be better than a drawer full of Farberware!*

•••

Don't give the squeaky wheel the grease. Give the grease to the one who is calm. This reinforces good behavior.

TIME AND TIME AGAIN TIME-OUTS

D on't use time-outs to discipline your children unless they are at least two years of age. Children younger than two typically do not understand language, have very short attention spans, and are naturally curious. If children younger than two misbehave, remove them from a situation, or redirect their energy.

• • •

Being consistent with time-outs and following through every day, every time, with each child can be emotionally and physically draining for the disciplining parent. You will sometimes find it much easier to give in than follow through with a time-out, particularly at the end of the day. Be consistent, but if you can't, realize that it's better to ignore a behavior than to warn of a punishment and not follow through. With multiples, "no" must mean "no."

...

Celebrate when they are good. Praise and reward them if the behavior warrants it. Since disciplining multiples can be exceptionally difficult when they misbehave, focus on good behavior whenever possible.

...

Don't feel the need to be in the middle of every disagreement. Sometimes it's better (and easier) to let siblings argue and work through their own differences.

...

If you need to give more than one time-out, avoid the subject of who started it. This will only cause more arguments. Also, be sure to separate your children when they are being disciplined.

...

Avoid spanking a child whenever possible. Take away a favorite toy instead.

...

Don't suggest a consequence that you are not willing to carry out (i.e., "If you do that, we won't go to Grandma's!"). In these cases, parents make mistakes because they only intend to warn, not discipline. Let your children know you are serious by choosing the consequences carefully.

...

Countdown from five, or something more appropriate, if you want them to respond to you. Simply telling them to do something sometimes doesn't work well without a time factor built in.

...

When a toddler throws food, take his plate away before a crumb reaches the floor and don't give it back. Doing this will teach him, as well as his sibling(s), a valuable lesson. If you give the plate back, this will also teach them a lesson!

...

Just when you think your toddler's behavior can't get any worse, he turns into an angel. As soon as this happens, it's his sibling's turn. Multiples seem to take turns with good and bad behavior and seem to "switch" every six months or so.

•••

When toddlers are bad, they can be really bad. They spit, hit, bite, kick, pull hair, and sometimes foam at the mouth in anger. When you get to this stage, you will have a practical understanding of the expression, "terrible twos"!

•••

"Put your own gas mask on first." When things heat up, they will only get worse if you are not in control. Control yourself before attempting to control anyone else.

•••

Do your best not to get aggravated over trivial things or punish when someone might not deserve to be punished. If you take a step back, you may discover your children have done nothing wrong. I'll never forget an incident I witnessed in a Dunkin Donuts parking lot. As I sat in my car, I watched a boy skip out of the shop and hand a donut to his mother. When the boy's mother saw the donut, she yelled, "You idiot! That wasn't the donut I wanted!" Think of the "mean mother" in the parking lot whenever you find yourself getting annoyed at some of the little things your children do. You will enjoy your children so much more if you learn to let them be young, immature, and allow them to make innocent mistakes.

•••

Whenever you discipline, remember the words of Henry Wadsworth Longfellow: "A torn jacket is soon mended; but hard words bruise the heart of a child." (Source: *www.storknet.com*)

•••

Some good news: Disciplining your multiples will become much easier as they learn more language and understand consequences. Remember to discipline them to the best of your ability. Someday they will be bigger than you, and they will always outnumber you!

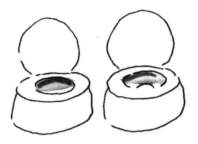

TOILET TRAINING TWINS OR TRIPLETS

Don't try to be the first one on your block to have your children potty trained. When you are a parent of multiples, it won't be worth the challenge. The longer you wait, the *easier* it will be!

• • •

Before you think about potty training your multiples, you will need to keep this in mind: Teaching your children to use the bathroom is not difficult. What makes potty training multiples a challenge is not the training itself, but the commitment required by parents. Potty training starts with parents as well as children. If you're not ready for potty training, your children will not be ready for potty training.

• • •

A commitment on behalf of the parents means that you are both willing to stop anything and everything you are doing to help your children get to, and use, the bathroom. A commitment means making your children's bathroom needs your number one priority. Interruptions in your daily

246 / *The Multiples Manual*

routine will happen all the time until your children can use the bathroom without your help. Getting your children to let you know that they have to use the bathroom will be relatively simple. When they do this, your children will be potty trained. Assisting them every time they have to use the bathroom will not be so simple.

•••

A commitment does not mean keeping your multiples in underwear until you go to the park, and then putting them in diapers. It means under-wear every day, all day (except for naps and bedtime to start). If you pick and choose when training is convenient, you will confuse your children and prolong the process.

•••

If you think you and your children are ready for training, ask yourself the following questions: 1) Are your children at least 2½ years old; 2) Are they able to "communicate"; 3) Are you and your spouse dedicated to potty training? If you answered "yes" to *all* of these questions, you are ready to give it a try.

•••

Although the thought of training two or three at a time can seem over-whelming, there is no need to read books that offer detailed instructions on how to train your children. Also, be aware of the fact that training multiple children is no different than training one child at a time, except that you will need two or three times the amount of patience.

•••

Sometimes parents experience a false start when their children are about 20 to 24 months of age. They encourage their children to use the bath-room because they can't wait to take diapers off their shopping list. Once their children finally "go," they race out to buy training pants and let the world know that their children are potty training. You can try training sooner if you feel your children are ready, but chances are it will involve more accidents, more time and effort, and in the long run, probably won't save you a nickel on diapers or other supplies.

•••

According to an article in *Parents Magazine*, a recent study of more than 250 toddlers performed by the Medical College of Wisconsin indicated that the median age to train girls is 34 months and boys is 36 months.

Note that these are median ages, meaning some train earlier than the median age, and some train later. Don't agonize if your children are not trained by the median age. It will happen!

• • •

With multiples, one child may be ready to train, while other(s) might not be. As the case study suggests, girls tend to be ready to train sooner than boys (although I have heard of many boys who had success before their sisters). If your toddlers are ready at the same time, train them together; if not, train them separately.

• • •

Avoid potty training during a transition period (going from a crib to a bed, a different bedroom, or anything else that might cause your children to feel anxious). Although these might not be such a big ordeal to you, they could be for your children. Take some time to think about events that might complicate or prolong the process before you move forward with your training.

• • •

When you have determined that your family is ready and have chosen a good start date (a weekend with no plans is good), talk to your children about the basics of using the bathroom. After your talk, take your potty trainees to a store (a day or two before training starts) to pick out their underwear. This gets them excited and gives them a sense of taking an active role in what is about to happen. When you buy underwear, buy at least six per child.

• • •

When you've chosen a good start date, you will need to test to make sure your children are truly "ready." When you do this, commit an entire day to putting them in their underwear (except for naps and night time). When they wake in the morning, remind them of what day it is, and let them use the bathroom. Let them sit for a minute or two and then get them dressed. If they go, praise them for their accomplishment and if they don't, thank them for their efforts.

• • •

Stay relaxed and optimistic, and don't waste your energy asking if they have to go every 15 minutes. As a general rule, ask every two hours. If they tell you they don't have to go, encourage them, but don't force them to use the bathroom. When one decides to use the bathroom and is successful, don't put that child on a different schedule. Stick to your two-hour intervals, whether they have gone or not. Repeat this throughout the day.

• • •

Expect that there will be accidents and be prepared for many clothing and underwear changes on the first day. When an accident happens, don't resort to diapers! Your children will need to experience a few accidents in order to understand what happens when they don't wear diapers. Accidents are part of the training process.

• • •

After you have endured an entire day without diapers, you will be able to determine which, if any, of your children are ready for another day of training. If a child had four or more accidents with no improvement throughout the day and no success on the toilet, he is not ready. Wait another month and repeat the process. If he is not ready a month later, wait another month and try again.

• • •

If you determine that one or more has control, repeat day one over again, this time focusing on those being trained. Again, expect that there will be accidents; and as long as they have fewer than four, they are doing well. You can offer stickers, M&Ms, or any other small reward every time they successfully use the bathroom, although an exaggeration of your pride is often enough.

• • •

Don't offer rewards for trying. Offer rewards for going. Although small treats or rewards will work well for the first day or two, they will probably be short-lived. When this happens, realize that your praise and encouragement will boost their confidence much more than any M&M ever will. Keep up with the praise and encouragement.

• • •

After a few days with minimal accidents, offer an incentive they can't resist (such as a visit to the toy store) if they can stay dry for five days. Let them know that you will start counting to five all over again if they have an accident (do this on an individual basis). Going any longer than five days might be unrealistic because they will continue to have occasional accidents. When you make it to day five, you will have successfully potty trained your children. Congratulations!

• • •

For the first couple of months, put your children in diapers for naps and at bedtime to avoid messes. As long as you make them aware that they only get a diaper during sleep time, the diapers should not confuse them.

• • •

Keep your children in diapers until they are dry for several nights in a row. When this happens, remove the diaper completely. If it has been a few months and your children still wet their diapers when they sleep, take away the diaper. You might find that they have control, but did not understand what was happening due to the absorbency of the diaper. *NOTE: Once they are trained, they will continue to occasionally wet their beds at night. This is common, and can last a few years.*

• • •

Many children master "peeing" before "pooping" on the toilet. This can occur for a couple of reasons: 1) This function usually takes longer for many children, and/or, 2) It might embarrass them. If this happens, give them privacy and accept that they will have a few messy accidents until they finally "go" on the toilet. If messy bowel movements are excessive, it's probably best to put the child(ren) back in diapers and try again in another month.

• • •

Training pants are expensive, glorified diapers. In my opinion, there is nothing more confusing to a child than a product that looks like underwear, but keeps him dry when he has an accident. Don't confuse your children with training pants. Stick to diapers until your children are ready to start using the bathroom.

• • •

Don't forget to protect mattresses with plastic mattress covers. If your children are restless sleepers, look for covers that wrap around the entire mattress (top and bottom). If your children are sound sleepers, keep it simple with fitted plastic top covers. When you're finished protecting your children's mattresses, remember to protect your own.

...

When it comes to potty training, the more toilets, the better. Buy a toilet seat insert as well as a potty seat for a bathroom you plan to use. If you have a two-story house, do the same in a bathroom on a different level.

...

Keep a potty seat in your car or minivan. Whether your trip is long or short, it will get used. Most parents with multiples keep one in their car out of necessity. It won't be the most pleasant thing to keep in your car, but it will be the most convenient! *NOTE: Look for the "On the Go Potty" by Kalencom* (www.kalencom.com).

...

Leave a few changes of clothing in your car at all times. This includes underwear, pants, socks and shirts. Remember to keep plastic bags handy for soiled clothing as well.

...

When your children are trained, get into the habit of asking them to "go" right before you leave the house. If they tell you they don't have to go, make them try. You will be amazed at what comes out of an empty bladder!

...

Avoid overalls and belts until your kids can help themselves in the bathroom. These are often the cause of accidents.

...

Potty training your kids can take six months or six days. This depends on the age of the children and whether or not they, as well as the parents, are ready. It does not depend on creative parenting techniques.

"I found potty training to be easiest during the summer months — less clothing to deal with."
— Linda B. (Mother of 4-year-old BB twins and a 7-year-old G singleton)

"At a very early age, I would tell my twins that after they used the toilet, it would be a good idea to 'wipe the rim and put the lid down.' I would also tell them 'they will make good husbands some day because their wives would really appreciate it.' Now, every time they go 'potty' they proudly announce that they 'wiped the rim and put the lid down.' Now that is what I call potty trained!"
— Kathy S. (Mother of identical twin boys and a daughter)

PRESCHOOL:
GETTING WAITLISTED

I f you plan to enroll your children in a preschool, start by doing your research and getting on a waiting list as soon as possible. It can be very difficult to find multiple spaces in a preschool of your choice. Getting on a list two years in advance is not unreasonable. It's better to be on top of a list than to wait and be on the bottom. Also, don't limit yourself to one list.

· · ·

Most parents find their multiples flourish in preschool, primarily for the following reasons:

- They offer much needed socialization with children other than their sibling(s).

- They offer lots of gross, fine motor, and other developmental activities.
- They tend to accentuate individuality, particularly when multiples form their own friendships, or thrive as individuals in separate classrooms.
- Reputable preschools usually do an excellent job preparing children for kindergarten.

• • •

There are a some drawbacks to enrolling your multiples in preschool, primarily:

- It can be cost prohibitive.
- Some mothers find it takes too much energy to get everyone ready and out the door, only to find that it's time to pick them up again (classes are usually about 2½ to 3 hours long).
- Children are exposed to more germs, and doctors' visits can become frequent and costly.

• • •

Many preschools offer sibling discounts, which is usually 10% off tuition for each additional sibling enrolled in the school. For example, if you enroll triplets, you would pay full price for the first child, take 10% off for the second child, and 10% off for the third.

• • •

Before you do any homework on preschools in your area, realize that one of the best ways to find out about their reputation is by word of mouth. Ask friends and neighbors in your area who have preschool age children for their opinions.

• • •

Review the following list of questions when interviewing a preschool director:

1) How much does their program cost and do they offer sibling discounts?
2) How many teachers and children are in each classroom and what is the teacher-to-student ratio?
3) Is the school state certified?

4) What are their screening procedures when hiring staff?

5) What is the average staff turnover rate?

6) How many preschool classes do they offer, and can you keep your children together, or separate them?

7) Can you tour the facility while classes are in session?

8) At what age do they enroll children into their program?

9) Do children need to be potty trained?

10) Do they provide lunch/snacks?

11) Do they have a waiting list?

12) Ask any other questions that may be important to you.

• • •

If you are not sure if you should keep your children in the same classroom or separate them, you are not alone. This is a much-discussed topic among parents of multiples, and no one seems to have a definitive answer. Think about what might be the best scenario for your children and ask that your children be placed accordingly. If you later find you don't like the arrangement, inquire about changing it.

"Do a 'dry run' before the first day of school to get an idea of how long it will take and where you are going." — Mary G. (Mother of 7-year-old GG twins, a 5-year-old G singleton, and 2-year-old BG twins)

SAVING FOR COLLEGES AND MORE

I f you plan to send your children to college, organizing your finances will be just as important as organizing your time. Don't forget, multiple births mean multiple college tuitions!

• • •

Saving for college is the inverse of potty training. The sooner you do it, the easier it will be. The savings you will need every month will grow exponentially if you wait. Start saving when your children are babies, even if the amount you can afford to put away each month is minimal. Doing this will save you a fortune in the long run.

• • •

An excellent way to start saving right away is by registering the credit cards you carry in your wallet with Upromise *(www.upromise.com)*. There is no fee to join. With Upromise, you can turn your everyday spending into college savings! When you register, every time you use your credit card for certain purchases you'll get a percentage of your spending back into your Upromise college savings account — automatically. You will find it well worth your time to find out more about this savings incentive program. There are no gimmicks and it's easy to sign up.

• • •

Before you make any purchases, look for a credit card that offers a choice of gift certificates or "rewards" instead of airline miles. Many of these cards offer gift certificates for Babies "R" Us, Baby Gap, Pottery Barn Kids, and much more. If you put everything you buy on this card, the rewards can be substantial. I have one of these cards, and at one point I had more than $1,000 in Baby Gap and Babies "R" Us gift certificates (I put a portion of my new minivan on my credit card)! When you have a card that offers rewards, be sure to register the card with Upromise. Doing this will give you rewards *and* savings for college! *NOTE: If you plan to put all of your purchases on your credit card, be sure to pay off the entire balance the following month. If you don't expect to pay the balance, don't use your card. Use checks or cash for your purchases and save money on interest payments.*

• • •

In order to organize your finances, develop a financial plan. List what you have now and figure out when and what you will need in the future. A financial advisor can help you develop a plan to accomplish your goals.

• • •

Prioritize your financial goals. Pay off credit card debt, consider consolidating and refinancing your mortgage, and start a regular savings program of monthly contributions into the most advantageous savings plan for you and your family. Also, consider making additional payments against your mortgage if your investments are not earning more than the interest rate on your mortgage.

• • •

Be sure to consider and understand the various savings plans available. These include custodial accounts, Education IRAs or Coverdell Education Savings Accounts, Section 529 Qualified Tuition Programs, and Qualified State Tuition programs. Do your homework before your children start doing theirs!

• • •

If you start saving for college when your children are young, the best way to save is by "dollar-cost-averaging." When you dollar-cost-average, you invest in certain equities every week, month, or six months over a number of years.

• • •

Take advantage of every tax-saving opportunity the Internal Revenue Service has to offer, including exclusions for each child, childcare deductions, childcare credits, and more. Look to the Internal Revenue Service website at *www.irs.gov* for more information, or better yet, meet with a tax professional to discuss tax-savings opportunities. Even if you have sufficient savings for your children's education, there are still tax-savings opportunities to take advantage of.

• • •

"Quicken Deluxe" software (about $50) is an excellent way to organize your personal finances. It manages your checkbook, reminds you when bills are due, and can even pay your babysitter and other bills online if you instruct it to! Quicken is also good for tracking where your money is going. You can purchase the software at *www.quicken.com* or at any store that sells software.

• • •

Sweat the small stuff if you are looking for ways to save more money. Pennies here and dollars there can add up when they are spent daily on small purchases. According to *Parents Magazine*, candy bars, treats for the kids, coffee breaks, vending machine snacks, and marathon phone calls can substantially add to your annual expenses.

• • •

If saving for college is not one of your immediate priorities, start praying for multiple scholarships!

"Start throwing pennies around like they're manhole covers if you plan to send your multiples to college."– My father, Richard C.

REASSURANCE AND POSITIVE THOUGHTS

Don't strive to be Martha Stewart's twin as you care for your children while they are young. Your children should be your priority, not your perfect cookies, tiered birthday cakes, and sculpted shrubbery. Happiness is being a mother with a realistic attitude, not a television version of what a perfect domestic engineer should be. When your cookies come out looking less than perfect, remember that Martha's would too, if she had young multiples, or even a singleton for that matter!

• • •

Always keep in mind that if someone is not walking in your shoes, they will have no right to critique you in any way. This will happen, but try your best not to let it bother you. Remind yourself that you are doing the best you can and that other mothers of multiples would say you deserve a medal for doing such a tremendous job. If you are not so sure, pick up the phone and call one!

• • •

Be the best you can be, and remember no one is perfect.

• • •

Take a moment every day to realize just how much you love your children. Then take another to realize just how much they love you.

• • •

Be thankful for laundry, it means you have loved ones nearby. (A quote from: *Lists to Live By*, by Alice Grav, Steve Stephens, and John VanDiest).

• • •

Don't view your house as being too small, think of it as easy to clean!

• • •

With multiples, an optimist always looks at a bottle as "half empty"!

• • •

Having a "bad day" will never even begin to compare to "any" day of infertility.

• • •

Thank God for the day that you have to spend with your children, and never lose sight of how fortunate you are.

• • •

Your kids will love you no matter what.

"Almost every day is hilarious when you have twins! You just need to take things in stride."
— Melissa B. (Mother of almost 3-year-old BB twins)

TIPS THAT WILL LAST A LIFETIME

My high school art teacher once taught me something I often think about in my daily experiences: One day I sat in class ready to give up on a painting I had been struggling with. My teacher sensed this and said, "Don't give up! Keep working on it! The more time you spend working on something, the better it gets." He encouraged me to continue, and I hesitantly took his advice. I worked and worked, until the painting was finished, and when I signed my name at the bottom I couldn't believe what a beautiful painting I had created. You're probably wondering, "What does a painting have to do with parenting multiples?" Not much, but the moral of this story is that you should never give up on anything you do, particularly with regard to your children. Every bit of effort you make will help to build your children's character and well-being. There will be many days where you will find yourself ready to give up, but if you stay focused and don't quit, you will soon realize that you are well on your way to creating a masterpiece. Or, in your case, two or three!

● ● ●

More recently, my kids' school principal said something I think is worth mentioning. As she addressed parents, she suggested that we look at school as "four walls with tomorrow inside." If you take a moment every day to view your home in the same way, it should give you an incredible sense of encouragement, and self-worth.

● ● ●

Go back in time to your childhood and think about the person who most positively influenced your life. Wouldn't it be nice if your children thought of *you* if they were ever asked this question?

● ● ●

"When you're good, good things happen. When you're bad, bad things happen." Repeat this daily if you want to emphasize a simple concept that works to reinforce good behavior.

● ● ●

It's easier to teach children to say, "May I please" than to get them to remember to say, "please" after every request. As an example, "May I please have a cookie?" is effortless, as compared to, "Can I have a cookie...please?" If you aren't sure, give it a try.

● ● ●

Teach your children to love and appreciate one another. Let them know that, "Friends will come and go, but their sibling(s) will always be there for them." A friend of mine, who happens to be a twin, shared this with me. He told me that this was the most valuable lesson his mother had ever taught him. Considering he's been married and divorced three times, I can understand why!

● ● ●

Begin and end every day with, "I love you!"

"Boys are more difficult than girls!"
— Words of wisdom from various mothers of multiple boys.

"Girls are more difficult than boys!"
— Words of wisdom from various mothers of multiple girls.

"The first 100 years are the hardest!" — Catherine M. (Mother of adult BB twins)

THINGS MOTHERS OF MULTIPLES WILL ONLY ADMIT TO OTHER MOTHERS OF MULTIPLES

They admit to being a bit envious of mothers with singletons, due to their seemingly effortless ability to get around with one child.

...

Mothers of multiples would sometimes rather not do something than pack everyone up in order to do it.

...

Many occasionally feel bored as a result of their inability to get out of the house as often as they once did.

• • •

Lots of them feel guilty for not doing enough with each child on an individual basis, or simply because they cannot do certain things with multiples. As a result, they feel as if they are "cheating" their children.

• • •

They sometimes resort to using the television as a babysitter.

• • •

A number of them admit they are more addicted to pacifiers than their children.

• • •

They occasionally put their babies to sleep with a bottle full of milk or formula, knowing very well they shouldn't do it. They do this as a last resort once exhaustion has taken over and nothing else has worked in getting their babies to sleep.

• • •

Nearly all of them prop bottles, and have numerous techniques. At the same time, they feel guilty about propping bottles.

• • •

Most find the dishwasher to be sufficient for cleaning bottles.

• • •

Some are embarrassed to admit this, but lots of them do it, and it saves them bundles of money: They put formula back into the refrigerator if a baby takes a sip of his bottle and decides he doesn't want any. *NOTE: If you do this, be sure to replace the bottle top with a clean cap and nipple, and refrigerate it right away. Feed the child with the same formula as soon as he decides he's ready for another bottle. You might think this is not a possibility now, but just wait. With multiples, this happens frequently. Pouring formula down the drain is like pouring liquid gold down the drain!*

• • •

To save time, they often use the same bowl and spoon to feed their multiples. To simplify things even more, they also feed right out of baby food jars, although baby books tell them not to.

• • •

They leave crumbs on the kitchen floor until the next meal.

...

It is not unusual for mothers to find the "cleanest" dirty clothes to dress themselves and their children, especially if there are only "a couple of spots on it."

...

Many mothers of multiples have a disorganized, or unkempt home when company is not present. I'll never forget one Thanksgiving dinner at my house. As soon as all of my company sat down to eat, my son asked, "Mommy, why is the house so clean?" I was so embarrassed, I felt like crawling into the turkey!

...

They admit to taking the stress from their day out on their husband as soon as he walks through the door at the end of a workday. Sometimes they give him five minutes and then unload!

...

While their children are babies, many would prefer to sleep than to be intimate with their spouses.

...

Many use prescription drugs to help them cope with stress, particularly during the infant stage.

...

They don't always shower everyday, and shave even less frequently.

...

Some admit to having a "favorite child." Some admit to having a favorite one month, and a different favorite the next!

...

If you do any or all of these, don't feel guilty. You are not alone!

"I remember feeling so guilty about propping bottles. All the parenting books talked about how it was 'bad.' I was so relieved at my first support group meeting when I found out most mothers of multiples propped bottles and their kids were all fine! Don't worry about propping bottles. Your children will grow up as normal functioning members of society!"
— Kathy R. (Mother of two sets of twins and a singleton)

"I wish I hadn't spent so much time feeling guilty."
— Numerous mothers of multiples whose children are now older.

WHY MULTIPLES
ARE EASIER THAN SINGLETONS

When you have multiples, you will learn that there really is safety in numbers. They look out for each other, and you can rest assured that they will always let you know when someone is up to no good!

• • •

When multiples are young, they can watch and rarely argue over the same television program or video. This is not usually the case with siblings of different ages.

• • •

You don't have to organize playgroups. You will already have one. However, being invited to one might be more of a challenge.

• • •

Once they are on a schedule, multiples generally take naps and go to bed at the same time. This is a great opportunity for mothers to regroup and take care of other responsibilities. This is not a possibility with a house full of singletons.

• • •

Since "misery likes company," doing things they don't necessarily want to do (like going to bed) is more acceptable to multiples. Peer pressure makes them conformists!

• • •

You can enroll them in the same activities for a number of years. This means running in fewer directions.

• • •

You can entertain the masses. Aside from gender-related toys, they tend to enjoy the same entertainment. For example, you can sing the ABCs and they will both/all learn from it, as well as enjoy it.

• • •

You don't have to be a short order cook. Children the same age generally eat the same things.

• • •

Hand me downs are a possibility with multiples! Many sets of them are slightly different sizes.

• • •

A stroller built for two or three is much more convenient than a stroller built for one with older singletons running in every direction in a shopping mall.

• • •

Parents of multiples can use assembly line techniques in just about everything they do with their children. At the end of the day, they often have it easier than parents of singletons because of all the short cuts and efficiencies they strive for, and become good at, on a daily basis.

• • •

One birthday party a year, one invitation mailing, and best of all, one set of thank you notes!

• • •

It is very convenient for parents to have best friends that live in the same house. They are a source of entertainment for each other.

•••

Two really is company, and three really is a charm…most of the time!

•••

My personal favorite: One pregnancy, and it's usually shorter than average!

"People always ask me, 'Triplets! How do you do it?' I always ask how they do it, because I can't imagine trying to accommodate the needs of multi-aged children. It has to be difficult. Having multiples is hard in the beginning, but once you pay your dues you get to reap the rewards!"
— Ellen M. (Mother of 6-year-old GGG triplets)

TIP # 1,002

Tip # 1,002 is a piece of advice that would truly simplify a mother of multiples' life. This tip is from my five-year-old triplet son, Jeffrey:

"You should only have one kid!"

When I jokingly asked him which three of my four children I should "give up," I was surprised that he didn't immediately point to his siblings. Instead, he thought for a minute and said, "Well, you have two arms and two legs, so can't you take care of all of us?" His reaction confirmed that he really enjoys being part of a group. This made me incredibly happy to be a mother to more-than-one, and grateful that my life is not so "simple" after all.

My wish for you is that you feel the same!

"Just when you think you have mastered all there is to know about a stage your children are in, they outgrow it and are on to another entirely new set of challenges!"
— Colleen S. (Mother of 7-year-old BGG triplets)

In memory of Kevin Smith
7/4/94–9/11/03

Kevin Smith and his identical twin Brian were the inspiration behind two of the tips that are published in this book. His mom, Kathy Smith, is a member and past president of the New Jersey Raritan Valley Mothers of Multiples.

Kevin's courage and grace were an inspiration to all those that knew him. He will live on in the hearts and minds of those whose lives he touched.

APPENDIX 1 —
REGISTRY CHECKLIST

TWINS / TRIPLETS REGISTRY CHECKLIST

	Should have?	Suggested quantity per child or in total:	Amount I think I will need:	Registered/ Bought Yes ( )	Price:	Brand(s) I am thinking about:	Found at Store/Website:
CLOTHING/COVER-UPS:							
clothing (easy on/off)	yes	Few to start					
onesies	yes	6 per child					
undershirts	yes	4 per child					
pair of socks (with elastic)	yes	5 per child					
sleeper outfits	yes	4–5 per child					
infant caps	yes	2–3 per child					
receiving blankets	yes	5–6 per child					
warm blankets	yes	1 per child					
jacket/bunting (fall/winter)	?	1 per child					
other							
TOILETRIES:							
shampoo (large bottle)	yes	1					
liquid bath soap	yes	2					
infant pain reliever (Tylenol)	yes	3					
infant gas drops (Mylicon)	yes	1					
diaper rash ointment	yes	1					
antibiotic cream	yes	1					
electrolyte solution (Pedialite)	yes	1					
rubbing alcohol	yes	1					
large bag cotton balls	yes	1					
large container Q-tips	yes	1					
fragrance/dye free laundry soap	yes	2					
baby powder	?	1					
baby lotion	?	1					
baby oil	?	1					
baby grooming kit	yes	1					
nasal bulb	yes	1					
thermometer	yes	1					
bathtub w/cushion	yes	1					
washcloths (adult-size)	yes	6 per child					
hooded bath towels	?	2 per child					
other							

TWINS / TRIPLETS REGISTRY CHECKLIST

	Should have?	Suggested quantity per child or in total:	Amount I think I will need:	Registered/ Bought Yes ( )	Price:	Brand(s) I am thinking about:	Found at Store/Website:
TRAVEL:							
stroller	yes	1					
infant car seats	yes	1 per child					
infant head supports/inserts	yes	1 per child					
baby carrier	?	1					
diaper bag	yes	1					
other							
ENTERTAINMENT/GEAR:							
activity pad/gymini	yes	1					
baby swing	yes	1					
vibrating bouncy seat	yes	1 per child					
bassinet	?	1 per child					
pack 'n play	?	1 per child					
playpen	?	wait to buy (if at all)					
other							
FEEDING (BOTTLE):							
formula	yes	wait to buy-ask pediatrician					
2 quart pouring pitcher w/ lid	yes	1 (if using powder)					
8 oz. bottles	yes	8 per child					
4 oz. bottles	yes	4 per child					
bottle brush	yes	1					
bottle drying rack	yes	1 (twins)/2 (trips)					
plastic dishwasher basket	yes	1(twins)/2 (trips)					
medium sized bibs (w/snaps)	yes	5 per child					
other							

TWINS / TRIPLETS LAYETTE CHECKLIST

	Should have?	Suggested quantity per child or in total:	Amount I think I will need:	Registered/ Bought Yes ( )	Price:	Brand(s) I am thinking about:	Found at Store/Website:
FEEDING (BREAST):							
double nursing pillow	yes	1					
double breast pump	?	1 (rent one)					
nursing bras	?	2–4 (wait until milk comes in)					
nursing t-shirt	yes	2–4					
nursing shawl	?	1					
nursing gown/button down	yes	2–4					
boxes – disposable nursing pads	yes	6					
jar/tube – nipple cream	yes	1					
cases – water bottles	yes	2					
vitamins	yes	ask consultant					
collection bottles/bags	?	ask consultant					
bottle nipples	?	ask consultant					
bottles	?	ask consultant					
other							
MISCELLANEOUS STUFF:							
memory book	yes	1 per child					
daily schedule book	yes	1					
pacifiers	yes	2 per child					
diaper pail	yes	2					
tall kitchen garbage bags	?	3–4 (if diaper pail uses them)					
diapers	yes	lots (newborn & size 1)					
case – baby wipes	yes	1					
burp cloths/cloth diapers	yes	8-10 per child					
other							
NURSERY:							
crib	yes	1 per child					
dresser	yes	1					
changing table	?	1					
glider/rocker	?	1–2					
ottoman	?	1					
small table	?	1					
other							

TWINS / TRIPLETS REGISTRY CHECKLIST

	Should have?	Suggested quantity per child or in total:	Amount I think I will need:	Registered/ Bought Yes ( )	Price:	Brand(s) I am thinking about:	Found at Store/Website:
CRIB:							
comforter/quilt	?	1 per child					
bumpers	?	1 per child					
skirt	?	1 per child					
fitted crib sheet	yes	2–3 per child					
crib mattress	yes	1 per child					
mattress cover	yes	1 per child					
sheet savers	yes	1–2 per child					
other							
OTHER NURSERY ITEMS:							
crib divider	?	1					
sleep positioner	yes	1 per child					
crib mobile	?	1					
musical sleep item	?	1					
crib mirror	?	1					
baby monitor	yes	1					
night light	yes	1					
humidifier	?						
clothes hamper	yes	1–2					
room darkening shades	?	1 per nursery window					
other							

APPENDIX 2 —
STROLLER MANUFACTURERS

✔ Check the box as you review each website, and highlight the sites with a marker if the company offers a stroller that interests you.
NOTE: Not all websites listed are ".com" Also, pricing is based on the company's stroller choices for MULTIPLES ONLY.

# SEATS			
1	2	3	4

STYLE		TYPE	
S	T	LTW	Lightweight
D	A	STD	Standard/Mid-Sized
BY	N	TRS	Travel System
S	D	UMB	Umbrella
D	E	VAR	Various Models
	M		

PRICES	
$	$100–200
$$	$201–300
$$$	$301–400
$$$$	$401–500
$$$$$	$501–600
$$$$$$	$601+

STROLLER MANUFACTURERS — Currently offering strollers for MULTIPLES

✔	1	2	3	4	Price Range	Manufacturer	Website	Customer Service	SBS	TND	Product(s)	Features/Comments
	•	•			$$$$$	Adv Buggy	abcbuggyusa.com	sales@abcbuggyusa.com	✔		ATR	Cool camouflage option. Toddler seat for 3rd child.
	•	•			$$$–$$$$$	Baby Jogger	babyjogger.com	(877) 241-1848	✔		JOG, ATR	Love the City Series! One second fold, rave reviews.
	•	•			$$$	Baby Planet	baby-planet.com	(877) 790-3113	✔		LTW	Modern. Easy steer handle.
	•	•			$–$$	Baby Trend	babytrend.com	(800) 328-7363		✔	VAR	SnapNGo — lightweight stroller frame for 2 car seats.
	•	•			$$–$$$$$	Bebe Love	bebeloveusa.com	(800) 832-2376	✔		ATR, JOG	DS Jogger — has all-pink and all-blue options.
		•	•		$$$$$–$$$$$$	Berg Design	bergdesign.net			✔	ATR	Some love it, some don't. May need hitch to transport.
	•	•			$$$	Bertini	bertinistrollers.com	(203) 348-7466	✔		ATR	Two bassinets available. Has a carriage-like look to it.
	•	•			$$$$–$$$$$	BOB Trailers	bobstrollers.com	(800) 893-2447	✔		ATR	Great for active parents.
	•	•			$	Chicco	chicco.com	(877) 4CHICCO	✔		UMB	Nice for quick trips and errands.
	•	•			$$	Combi	combi-intl.com	(800) 992-6624	✔		STD	Great for shopping. Attractive, modern design.
	•	•			$	Compass	compassbaby.com	(888) 899-2229		✔	STD	Lightweight, quick fold, stadium seating.
	•	•			$$–$$$	Double Decker	doubledeckerstroller.com	(239) 543-1582		✔	TRS	Accomodates 2 & 3 car seats.
	•	•			$$$–$$$$	Drm Design	dreamerdesign.net	(800) 278-9626	✔		ATR, JOG	A funky twist on a jogger. Good for active parents.
	•	•			$$$$$	Easy Walker	easywalker.nl	31 (0) 294 230 351	✔		ATR	Limited distribution in the US, interesting colors.
	•	•			$	Evenflo	evenflo.com	(800) 233-5921		✔	STD	Stadium seating, snack tray. Inexpensive, no frills stroller.
	•	•	•		$$–$$$$	Foundations	foundations.com	(330) 722-5033	✔		STD, UMB	Triple — Great stroller for the $. Limited seat recline.
	•	•			$–$$	Graco	gracobaby.com	(800) 345-4109	✔		STD	Very popular and practical. Some models fit 2 car seats.
	•	•			$$	In Step	instep.net	(800) 242-6110	✔		JOG	Great stroller for the price. Little sun protection.
	•	•	•		$$–$$$$$$	Inglesina	inglesina.com	(877) 486-5112	✔		VAR	Domino Trio — may have to disassemble to fit in car.
	•	•			$	Jmason	jmason.com	(800) 242-1922		✔	STD, UMB	Very lightweight umbrella strollers.
	•	•			$$$$$	Jane	janeusa.com	(866) 355-2630	✔		ATR	Modern design. Tight space in back.
	•	•	•		$$–$$$	Joovy	joovy.com	(877) 456-5049		✔	UMB, TRS	Big Caboose — fits 2 car seats w/platform for 3rd child.
	•	•			$$$	Kelty	keltykids.com	(800) 423-2320	✔		JOG	Double joggers — too wide for standard doorways.
	•	•			$$$	Knuckle Head	knuckleheadsports.com	sales@knuckleheadsports.com	✔		JOG	Traditional jogging strollers.

STROLLER MANUFACTURERS — Currently offering strollers for MULTIPLES (continued)

✓	1	2	3	4	Price Range	Manufacturer	Website	Customer Service	SBS	TND	Product(s)	Features/Comments
	•	•			$	Kolcraft/Jeep	kolcraft.com	(800) 453-7673	✓	✓	STD, UMB	Tandem — one hand fold, snack tray. Fits 1 car seat.
	•	•			$$$$	Kool Stop	koolstop.com	(800) 586-3332	✓		JOG	Traditional jogging strollers.
	•	•			$$$	LL Bean	llbean.com	(800) 441-5713	✓		JOG	Black only. Holds passengers up to 50 pounds.
	•	•			$$-$$$	Maclaren	maclarenbaby.com	(877) 442-4622	✓		UMB	Very popular, modern, higher-end umbrella strollers.
	•	•			$$$$$	Motobecane	motobecane.com	info@motobecane.com	✓		JOG	Fits through doorways. Limited colors.
	•	•	•		$$$$$-$$$$$$	Mnt Buggy	mountainbuggy.com	(866) 524-8805	✓		ATR	Rugged, perfect for "outdoorsy" parents.
	•	•	•		$$-$$$$$$	Peg Perego	pegperego.com	(800) 671-1701	✓	✓	VAR	Fits 2 & 3 car seats. Great for newborn and older babies.
	•	•			$$$-$$$$$	Phil & Teds	regallager.com	(800) 593-5522	✓	✓	ATR	Many color options. Both styles fit through doorways.
	•	•			$	Safety 1st	safety1st.com	(800) 544-1108		✓	LTW, STD	Dual facing. Accommodates 2 infant car seats.
	•	•	•		$$-$$$$	Safetech	chapmansitplus.com	chapmansplus@aol.com	✓		JOG	More economical jogging strollers.
	•	•			$$$$$	Stroll-Air	stroll-air.com	(519) 579-4534	✓		ATR	Fits 2 car seats w/adapter. Dual facing.
	•	•			$$$-$$$$	Tike Tech	tiketech.com	(800) 296-4602	✓		ATR, JOG	Joggers are a good value for the price.
	•	•			$$$$$$	Valco	valcobaby.com	(800) 610-7850	✓		ATR	Offers toddler seat for 3rd child.
	•	•			$$$	Zooper	zooper.com	(888) 742-9899	✓		STD	Some claim not enough seat separation.
	•	•				BeBeCar	bebecar.com	info@bebecar.com	✓	✓	STD	Sold outside the US
	•	•				Cosatto	cosatto.com	0870 050 5900	✓	✓	LTW, UMB	Sold outside the US
	•	•				Emmaljunga	emmaljunga.com	Visit site for retailer #	✓		ATR	Sold outside the US
	•	•				First Wheels	firstwheels.nl	31 0 20 6304887	✓		ATR	Sold outside the US
	•	•				I'coo	hauckuk.com	01 (0) 9057 608 003			ATR	Sold outside the US
	•	•	•			Kidz Kargo	kidzkargo.co.uk	info@kidzkargo.co.uk	✓	✓	ATR, UMB	Sold outside the US
	•	•	•	•		Lots of Babies	lotsofbabies.com	0161 740 9979	✓	✓	VAR	Sold outside the US
	•	•				LoveNCare	lovencare.ie	087 9005650	✓		JOG	Sold outside the US
	•	•				Mutsy	mutsy.com	Contact via website		✓	ATR	Sold outside the US
	•	•				Red Castle	redcastle.fr	Contact via website	✓		ATR	Sold outside the US

✓ Check the box as you review each website.
NOTE: Prices are not listed for single strollers.

# SEATS			
1	2	3	4
S	S	S	S
	E	E	E
S	A	A	A
E	T	T	T
A	S	S	S
T			
S			

PRICES	
$	$100–200
$$	$201–300
$$$	$301–400
$$$$	$401–500
$$$$$	$501–600
$$$$$$	$601+

STYLE	
S	T
D	A
BY	N
S	D
D	E
	M

TYPE	
LTW	Lightweight
STD	Standard/Mid-Sized
TRS	Travel System
UMB	Umbrella
VAR	Various Models

STROLLER MANUFACTURERS — Currently offering strollers for SINGLETONS

✓	1	2	3	4	Price Range	Manufacturer	Website	Customer Service	SBS	TND	Product(s)	Features/Comments
	•					Britax	britaxusa.com	(888) 427-4829			VAR	Single only
	•					Bugaboo	bugaboo.com	Contact via website			ATR	Due out with a double in 2008
	•					Bumble Ride	bumbleride.com	(800) 530-3930			ATR, STD	Single only
	•					Cosco	coscojuvenile.com	(800) 544-1108			LTW, UMB	Single only
	•					Eddie Bauer	djgusa.com	(800) 544-1108			STD	Single only
	•					Englacha	englachausa.com	(626) 335-5961			ATR	Single only
	•					Fisher-Price	fisher-price.com	(800) 432-5437			ATR, STD	Single only
	•					Go-Go Babyz	gogobabyz.com	(888) 686-2552			ATR	Single only
	•					Mia Moda	miamodainc.com	(866) MIA-MODA			STD	Single only
	•					Orbit	orbitstrollers.com	(877) ORB-BABY			ATR	Single only
	•					Rock Star Baby	rockstarbaby.com	Contact via website			ATR	Single only
	•					Silver Cross	silvercrossamerica.com	(858) 587-4745			VAR	Single only
	•					Stokke	stokkeusa.com	(877) 978-6553			ATR, TRS	Single only
	•					UPPA Baby	uppababy.com	(800) 760-2060			ATR, UMB	Single only
	•					Icandy	icandyuk.com	44 (0) 1462 484 858			ATR, STD	Sold outside the US
	•					Micralite	micralite.com	44 (0) 1892 615 900			ATR	Sold outside the US
	•					Quinny	quinny.com	020 8236 0707			ATR, UMB	Sold outside the US

WEBSITE LISTINGS

INDEX

....

Additional copies of

The Multiples Manual

can be purchased online at:

www.justmultiples.com

For wholesale pricing,
please send an e-mail to:

justmultiples@yahoo.com